# THE
# URBAN
# PREPPER'S
# GUIDE

## DISCLAIMERS

The content of this book, including discussion of possible legal issues, is centered on a basic understanding of the laws in the United States. It is incumbent upon each reader to do their own research on the laws, statutes, and ordinances that may be in effect where they live, work, and recreate. Don't risk a lot for a little. Meaning, there is almost always a legal way to accomplish a given goal, if you're willing to put in the work to make it happen. Looking for shortcuts isn't wise. You could end up paying fines with money you could have used for prepping. That said, absolutely nothing in this book should be considered legal advice. Instead, seek the counsel of an attorney with whom you've entered into a retainer agreement.

In regards to any medical-related information contained in this book, always seek professional medical advice and treatment from competent and licensed providers.

Products mentioned throughout the book are mostly from manufacturers located in the United States. However, their products are generally available anywhere. If you are unable to source them locally, you can probably find suitable replacements with the information provided herein relating to the product specifications.

Published in 2022 by Welbeck
an imprint of Welbeck Non-Fiction Limited,
part of Welbeck Publishing Group.

Based in London and Sydney
www.welbeckpublishing.com

A CIP catalogue record for this book is available from the British Library.

ISBN 978-1-78739-835-1

Printed in Dubai

10 9 8 7 6 5 4 3 2 1

MIX
Paper | Supporting responsible forestry
FSC® C004800
www.fsc.org

# THE
# URBAN
# PREPPER'S
# GUIDE

## HOW TO BECOME
## SELF-SUFFICIENT AND PREPARED
## FOR THE NEXT CRISIS

### JIM COBB

WELBECK

"Jim Cobb is the voice of reason and experience with all things survival. If he says something works, then you know you're getting solid, field-tested information from a respected leader in the survival industry who is constantly applying his skills and incorporating what he teaches into his daily life. Jim is the go-to guy for learning how to prepare for an urban disaster so you and your family can prevail through an unexpected emergency."

TONY NESTER,
Author of the
*Knife-Only Survival Book*

"Jim Cobb is a master at what it takes to survive in the city or anywhere. He provides you with the basic skills and knowledge for handling challenging situations ethically, with the big picture in mind. Jim gives you the tools and the knowledge for finding your path of self-reliance, for surviving with a smile when others are panicking."

CHRISTOPHER NYERGES,
author of *How To Survive Anywhere*

"Jim Cobb is one of the most practical, no-nonsense preparedness authors around. You can always count on him to cut through the nonsense of unrealistic advice and boil it down to logical, down-to-earth steps that will work for anyone. The survival world sincerely needs a book that was written for preppers living in urban and suburban areas, and this book promises to offer solid gold advice."

DAISY LUTHER,
founder of TheOrganicPrepper.com

"Jim is the author you read when you want no-nonsense preparedness and survival. You won't find myths and unproven tactics in his writings, just practical advice you can put to good use!"

TODD SEPULVEDA,
host of The Prepper Website Podcast

# CONTENTS

# INTRODUCTION

**WHEN YOU READ OR HEAR THE WORD "PREPPER," WHAT COMES TO MIND? HOW ABOUT IF WE CHANGE IT TO "SURVIVALIST"? FOR MANY, THOSE WORDS HAVE SOMETHING OF A NEGATIVE CONNOTATION, WITH IMAGES OF KOOKS WEARING TIN-FOIL HATS AND EATING MILITARY RATIONS IN A BASEMENT. I'LL BE HONEST: I'VE BEEN AROUND THE SURVIVAL COMMUNITY FOR MORE THAN 30 YEARS AND, WELL, THERE ARE INDEED A FEW WHO FIT THAT MOLD.**

However, the vast majority of preppers are just normal folk who desire to be better prepared for emergencies. For most of them, this is simply common sense.

It might be helpful if we take a quick look at how we got to where we are today.

### HISTORY OF PREPPING

Being prepared for emergencies is hardly a new concept, despite the bad press it gets from time to time. The so-called Prepping Movement has gone through a few different iterations over the years.

Over the years, many within the survival and preparedness community talk about how this is just how people lived back in the day, planning ahead to make it through the year. While true, I

contend that prepping, at least in a semblance we'd recognize as such today, didn't really begin until the early 1940s. To my way of thinking, there's a difference between putting food up in fall because otherwise you will quite literally starve to death as there are no other options for sustenance, and taking measures specifically toward mitigating potential disasters that could occur.

It was in 1941 that President Franklin D. Roosevelt created the Office of Civilian Defense. The purpose was to coordinate efforts to protect citizens against attack during wartime. One of the tasks was to establish the United States Citizens Defense Corps. Millions of people were trained in a variety of essential duties, from providing first aid to decontaminating after a chemical attack.

Civil defense changed as time went on, shifting more toward the threat of nuclear attack. Bomb shelters became popular, with various government agencies providing information and resources to communities on how to best handle this kind of emergency. There were "duck and cover" drills conducted in schools regularly.

But by the 1970s, formal civil defense was beginning to wane. In 1979, the Defense Civil Preparedness Agency, the latest incarnation of the Office of Civilian

Defense, was disbanded and replaced by the Federal Emergency Management Agency (FEMA). The role of FEMA was geared toward providing direct support and aid when disasters occurred. Following the attacks on 9/11, FEMA was rolled into the Department of Homeland Security.

## THE RISE OF THE SURVIVALIST

Okay, let's back up just a touch on the timeline. Beginning in the late 1960s, public trust in the government had begun to falter. Some people felt that they couldn't or shouldn't rely on federal or state agencies to protect them. In fact, some of those folks feared that it was the government itself that was the largest threat.

Kurt Saxon was an author who wrote several books, such as *The Poor Man's James Bond*, that discussed improvised weapons and explosives. In the mid-1970s, he began a newsletter called "The Survivor". In it, he talked extensively about homesteading, pioneer skills, and similar topics. Along the way, he also coined the term "survivalist," using it to refer to those who were taking steps toward being more self-reliant.

Not long after "The Survivor" began, Mel Tappan started publishing his own newsletter, calling it the

"Personal Survival ("P.S. Letter"). A number of prominent members of the survivalist community contributed articles, including Colonel Jeff Cooper and Dr. Bruce D. Clayton. In large part, the focus of the "P.S. Letter" was on establishing a survival retreat, a place you could escape to if things got bad and which you could stockpile with all manner of food and supplies. And again, one of the biggest threats they saw was from our own government. That concern wasn't without cause either, given what later happened at Ruby Ridge, Waco, and other places.

With the arms race ramping up between the United States and the Soviet Union, interest in survival planning was also on the rise through the 1980s and into the early 1990s. Then, as we approached the new millennium, the dreaded Y2K bug began to be discussed. Suddenly families across the country were flocking to stores to buy all kinds of disaster supplies, just in case when the clock hit midnight on New Year's Eve in 1999 all of the computers in the world went haywire.

## FROM SURVIVALIST TO PREPPER

While Y2K turned out to be nothing, it is notable for another reason. This is when preppers first began to develop and differentiate from the survivalists. Where the survivalists were concerned with world-altering events such as a full-blown nuclear war, other folks were more worried about incidents such as natural disasters, bad weather, even job loss.

It was in the early 2000s that the term "prepper" began to be used to describe these people. Some might call the approach survivalist-lite. Instead of having a primary interest in heading for an off-grid survival retreat at the first sign of trouble, the preppers wanted to learn how to shelter in place at home. Instead of learning how to build improvised explosives, they wanted to learn how to grow a garden in the backyard.

After the 9/11 attacks and the establishment of the U.S. Department of Homeland Security, even the government got into the act, recommending citizens put together emergency kits for their homes and vehicles. Along the way, the dividing line between the two camps, survivalists and preppers, began to get muddied, in large part due to the media. They used the terms interchangeably, regardless of who they were talking about, and it didn't take long before the general public saw no difference between the two either.

Depending upon the source you consult, there are anywhere from 5 to 10 million people in the United

States who are actively taking steps to be better prepared for disasters. After the COVID-19 pandemic and resulting issues affecting everything from public health policies to supply shortages, I think it is safe to say that that number will continue to climb.

As more and more people embrace the idea, even if they don't quite think of themselves as true preppers just yet, many of them are wondering, "Where do I start?"

Here, right here, is where you begin. The goal of *The Urban Prepper's Guide* is to show you how to be ready for the next disaster, using logic and a down-to-earth approach. We're not talking about investing in a massive secret retreat in the middle of nowhere or stocking up on enough armaments to take over a Third World country. Just simple things anyone can do that will put them in a much better position when negative events take place.

Time and again on social media I've seen questions from city residents, asking for advice and guidance on how to prep when you live in an urban or suburban area. The standard, and shortsighted, answer from many is just to move out of the city. I consider that to be dodging the question. It just isn't practical, feasible, or frankly desirable for everyone to live out in the sticks, away from the hustle and bustle.

While a city isn't the best place to be during a disaster, the situation isn't as hopeless or dire as others may predict. There are, in fact, many things you can do as an urban resident who wants to be prepared, from building up a stockpile of food and other supplies to strengthening your security measures to protect what you have.

We face an endless array of potential crises, from unexpected job loss to natural disasters large or small. If 2020 taught us anything, it is that we can never know what the next day will bring. While we might not know precisely what the future holds, common sense tells us that it won't all be roses and sunshine. That's not being negative, just realistic.

It's important to remember that I can only do so much. I can provide you with information and advice, guidance and support, but it is up to you to do something with it. Don't let this be just a passing fancy. Take the next step and set a goal to be better prepared, then work just a little bit each day toward getting there.

Enjoy the journey toward self-reliance!

# CHAPTER 1
# WATER

**IT BEGINS WITH WATER. WHETHER YOU WANT TO CALL IT PREPPING, "SURVIVALISM", OR JUST COMMON SENSE, THE FIRST KEY ELEMENT IS WATER. WHILE VARIOUS EXPERTS, ONLINE AND IN PRINT, WILL STATE ONE CAN SURVIVE UPWARD OF THREE DAYS WITHOUT WATER, THAT'S ACTUALLY PRETTY POSITIVE THINKING. MANY FACTORS COME INTO PLAY TO AFFECT THAT TIME FRAME, INCLUDING CLIMATE, PHYSICAL FITNESS, AND EXERTION LEVEL.**

Water isn't just for consumption, of course. We use it for a ton of things. Have you ever kept track of how much water your family uses in a day? From drinking and food prep to flushing toilets, washing dishes, bathing, and laundry, just one person can easily go through 80+ gallons (800+ liters) a day. And that's not counting watering the yards or the pets. While some of those activities might be reduced or even eliminated during a major disaster, many of them are critical to survival. The point is that we tend to use an awful lot of water without giving it much thought.

Easy access to clean water is often one of the first things to go in the wake of a major disaster. Fortunately, there are several things we can do to prepare for one.

## CONSERVATION

In a short-term emergency, it should be quite easy to decide that laundry and some other water-related chores can be delayed for the time being. The primary focus is ensuring there is enough water to drink, use for cooking, and some limited dish washing. A full shower or bath can wait until after the crisis has passed.

The first rule, and probably the one that will be the hardest for many to follow initially, is to never let a single drop of water go to waste.

Here's just one example. Let's say you invested in a camp shower. These handy pieces of gear consist of a black plastic bag that you fill with water and suspend from a tree branch or perhaps a tall ladder.

Being dark colored, it absorbs the sun's rays and heats the water inside. You then use the attached hose and nozzle to bathe. It is a good piece of equipment to have. Pick up or scrounge a plastic or metal tub in which you'll stand as you use the shower. A child's pool works great, if you can find one. All of the water you use gets collected in the bottom of the tub. When you're done showering, toss some dirty clothes into the bottom of the tub and do a little laundry. Once that's done, pour the water into the flower bed. Get as much use as you can out of every single drop. You might not be able to take a long, lingering hot shower, much less a bath, but you can clean up fairly well with even just a little water.

The second rule will be fairly easy if you're in a position where you're hauling water by hand. Prioritize what truly needs to be done with the limited water you have.

Consumption should always come first. We often think of dehydration as something that is relegated to times of hot weather and heavy exertion. While those factors do increase the risk, the fact is many people are at least mildly dehydrated on a daily basis. Few of us really buckle down and drink as much water as our bodies need. That will be even more difficult to do when supplies are limited.

After consumption, the next priority is on hygiene, such as frequent hand washing. We'll dive further into this later, but illness can spread quickly throughout a home and community when hygiene isn't kept up properly.

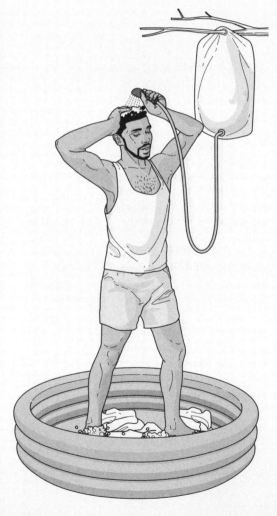

## STOCKPILING

Several sources recommend that a minimum of 1 gallon (3.75 liters) of water per person per day of the disaster will be needed. I've always had issues with that line of thinking. For starters, how in the world can we possibly know ahead of time how long a given crisis might last? For an average family of four, we're talking 28 gallons, per week. Okay, that's not too bad but, when we look at it as 120 gallons (454 liters) a month, that's when it starts to get a little tricky.

Water is what it is, meaning it takes up a certain amount of space and weighs a certain amount. One gallon of water takes up 231 cubic inches (3.8 cu m) and weighs 8 ½ pounds. Those two facts are immutable. You can't make water lighter and you can't compress it into a smaller space. It is what it is.

This leads to serious problems if you want to stockpile a large amount of water. I've heard some people store 55-gallon (208-liter) drums of water in the basement. That's great but those barrels aren't going anywhere once they're full. That's 458 pounds (208 kg) of water in each barrel. Hopefully, those who use this approach to water storage think ahead and install taps on the barrels, and keep the barrels on risers for easy access.

Apartment and condo residents don't have the luxury of a large basement they can use for storage, either. Putting a half ton of water in your spare bedroom might not work out well. For reference, a king-size waterbed holds about 235 gallons (890 liters) and landlords have traditionally been reluctant about them as it is, let alone doubling or quadrupling the amount of water being kept in one spot.

There are various containers that are designed for storing water. Just one example is the Aqua-Tainer. It holds up to 7 gallons (26.5 liters). Another is the Water Brick, which holds 3 ½ gallons (13.25 liters) and stacks together like building blocks. If you go the route of bulk storage using one or another of these types of containers, be sure you'll be able to lift and move it once it is full. Most people could probably handle the Water Brick at just shy of 12 pounds. A fully loaded Aqua-Tainer, though, weighs almost 60 pounds (27 kg).

Another consideration with bulk containers is how the water is dispensed. Many of them have some kind of tap, either built in or as an accessory. It is a desirable feature becuase it prevents you from having to lift the container and pour the water out. Instead, you can keep the container on a counter or table and dole out the water as necessary.

If you're on municipal water, it has already been treated at the plant and should be just fine to store without adding anything to it. Otherwise, add a few drops of nonscented chlorine bleach to the water before closing up the container. It will kill off any lingering microscopic organisms that could cause you to have a bad day.

I recommend rotating water stored in these bulk containers. Meaning, use it up and refill the containers, preferably about twice a year. This ensures the water will be fresh when you need it. Use the water for consumption, pets, or plants instead of just pouring it down the sink. Water is a precious resource and should never be wasted. Inspect the container each time you've emptied it. Look for mold inside and out, as well as inspect the condition of the container itself. Discard any that are cracked or are close to cracking.

The other popular method of water storage for long-term use is to purchase bottled water by the case. I'm old enough to remember when buying bottled water was something only the wealthy did, for the most part. It was even a subject for stand-up comedy routines back then. Obviously, times have changed.

I can easily pick up a case of 24 half-liter bottles with my regular food shopping. That's roughly 3 gallons of water. Cases of water stack pretty well, especially if you do crisscross layers of two side by side. They are easy to carry. On top of that, commercially bottled water has been sealed in such a way that it will remain potable for years, provided the seal isn't broken.

Using our example of a family of four, if each case amounts to about

# STORAGE GUIDELINES

No matter how much water you store or how you go about it, there are a few basic rules to follow.

1   Store the water where it is easily accessible, keeping in mind its weight. For example, I don't recommend setting up several 55-gallon (208-liter) drums of water in an upstairs bedroom. That much weight concentrated into a small area of floor is asking for trouble.

2   Don't store water containers directly on concrete, because there are reports that indicate there can be some leaching of chemicals from the floor getting into the water. Put the containers on wood pallets, if possible.

3   Keep the water in a cool, dark place. Avoid direct sunlight, which can negatively impact the plastic containers. Heat can also cause similar problems.

3 gallons, they'll need to store about 10 cases for each week of the crisis. Not too difficult to do to prep for a week or two but prepping for several weeks will take up some serious floor space. However, even in a small apartment, there is some amount of closet space that can be used, along with stashing a few cases under beds.

Remember, too, that all of those numbers are predicated upon an average of 1 gallon of water per person per day. That's just barely subsistence levels of hydration in many cases. Sure, in the middle of winter, when most of the time is spent indoors, 1 gallon might suffice. However, in the middle of summer, when everyone is working in the yards not so much.

Regardless of climate and workload being performed, 1 gallon per day won't allow for much of any bathing, not to mention laundry, pets, plants, and other areas of life that need water.

Look at water storage as a stopgap measure. In other words, the water you store in cases and bulk containers in the basement or under beds is for the short-term, to get you over the hump while you implement more sustainable kinds of solutions. Store as much water as is feasible for your family, but recognize that you'll never be able to store enough for a long-term scenario.

## OUTSIDE SOURCES

### SWIMMING POOLS

At first, it is an appealing thought. The average above-ground swimming pool holds about 5,000 gallons (18,930 liters). An in-ground model holds even more. If you have kids, we're disregarding the potential amount of urine in the pool and just calling it all water. So, let's say you splurged your tax return on one of those quick-set above-ground pools. You maintain it faithfully with shock and keep it clean with skimmers. You figure that at any given time, during pool season at least, you have enough water to last you and your family for a few months.

Pools are treated with chlorine on a regular basis. That's what prevents the growth of algae and other things we generally see as undesirable in water in which we're about to frolic. Chlorine is also added to our tap water to ensure it is safe to drink. Even the amounts are similar. Municipalities tend to shoot for a chlorine concentration of about 1-1.5 ppm (parts per million). A healthy swimming pool runs about the same, 1.0-3.0 ppm. So far, so good, right?

Here's the thing. It isn't the chlorine in the pool water that is the problem, it is the stabilizers, algaecides, and other chemicals included with the chlorine when it is added to the pool. These chemicals prevent the chlorine from dissipating as quickly as it normally would, allowing it to stay in the water and do the job of killing anything nasty. While ingesting some chlorine probably won't hurt you, not at the levels we're discussing anyway, those other chemicals aren't good for you. A swallow of pool water here and there when you're practicing your underwater handstands is one thing. Consuming several glasses of it throughout the day is another thing.

Boiling, as we'll discuss later, is one of the most common and most reliable methods of water disinfection. In this case, however, you'd actually end up doing more harm than good. When water is boiled, a percentage of it is lost as steam. Those harmful chemicals are left behind. The end result is you'd be concentrating the level of chemicals in the water.

You could eliminate the problem by only using nonscented chlorine bleach in your swimming pool. This is an approach many use and reports are generally positive. However, I doubt many pool manufacturers would recommend that course of action. It comes down to a judgment call on your part. Using no other pool chemicals can lead to algae growth and other issues. Even if the water remains crystal clear, I'd still want to filter it, just in case.

## RAINWATER

One of the easiest ways to collect water is to set up rain barrels. Hundreds of gallons of water can be collected in just one rainstorm, so it would be foolish not to take advantage of this resource. I'd encourage you to get rain catchment systems up and running sooner rather than later. The system doesn't need to be overly complicated. Just install rain gutters on your home and have barrels set up at each downspout. If you have outbuildings such as detached garages or large sheds, see about installing gutters and rain barrels for them as well.

A cistern is basically a giant rain barrel. The gutter system on the home or building directs the water into these large, sealed containers instead of individual barrels. A cistern is a great advantage in a long-term crisis but, because of their size, they can be obvious even to the casual observer when they are located above ground. Installing one below ground can be a pricey endeavor.

Water collected through any rainwater catchment systems will still need to be filtered and disinfected

prior to consumption. While rain is generally pure as it falls from the sky, it can and will be contaminated by whatever it lands on.

## WATER IN THE WILD

In many areas of the world, one is rarely too far from some body of water, whether it be a river, stream, pond, or lake. These are all good sources for water, provided you have the means to filter and disinfect it. However, the dangers from drinking contaminated water cannot be overstated. All waterborne illnesses will cause dehydration due to the fluid being lost from vomiting and other symptoms. Think about it like this. If water is in limited supply, do you really want to have to try to clean up after someone has been seriously ill, possibly for several days?

Assume all water collected in the wild is contaminated, no matter how clear it is or how fast it is running downstream. This goes double for water obtained from urban parks and public areas, because the grass around it will probably have been treated with chemicals that then run off into the pond. Make sure the treatment method you choose to use for water contaminated in this way will remove the pesticides and such.

# QUICK RAIN
## CATCHMENT

If you lack the ability to set up gutters and rain barrels, all is not lost. You can still collect a reasonable amount of rainwater with minimal effort. My good friend John McCann at Survival Resources (SurvivalResources.com) showed me an easy way to collect rainwater. It is a great standalone solution as well as an excellent way to augment your existing rainwater catchment system.

Purchase or scrounge four metal fence posts, the type often used for temporary fencing. You'll also need a tarp, sledgehammer, some cordage, and several buckets.

Select a location that is out in the open, away from trees that might block rainfall. Lay the tarp on the ground. For our example here, we'll say the tarp is 8 x 10 feet (2.4 x 3 m). Pound one post in at each of two corners on the short side of the tarp. Make sure you drive the posts in far enough to be stable. Use lengths of cordage to tie the tarp corners to the posts about 4 feet (1.2 m) from the ground.

Move to the opposite end of the tarp. Drive the remaining two fence posts in at spots a couple of feet (60 cm) in from the long sides of the tarp. When you tie these corners to the posts, it will create a funnel shape. Tie the corners to the posts at spots lower than the previous two posts. You want the end of the funnel to be about 24-30 inches (60–75 cm) from the ground.

Position your bucket under the end of the funnel. Use some cordage to tie a fist-size rock to the funnel, with the cordage being left long enough so the rock just rests on the bottom of the bucket. When the rain comes, be ready with extra buckets because they will fill quickly. You'll harvest far more rainwater using this tip than you will by just placing empty containers out on the ground during a rainstorm.

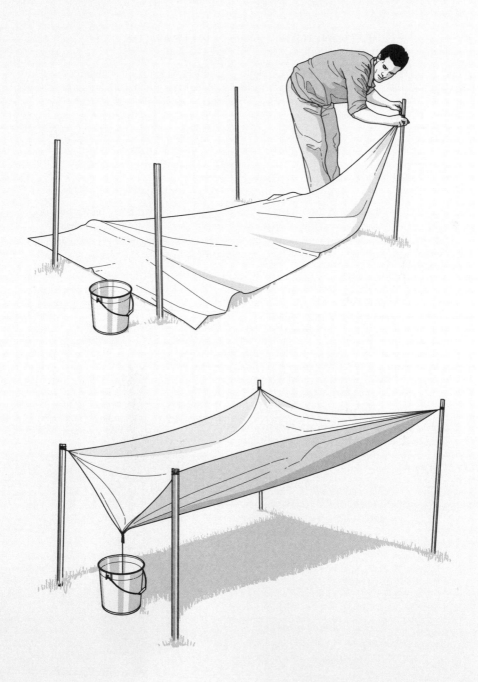

## FILTRATION AND DISINFECTION

Unless you are absolutely certain the water is potable, you will need to filter and/or disinfect it prior to consumption or using it for food preparation. Neglecting this step can lead to serious illness or worse.

Cryptosporidium and giardia are two protozoa that may be present in questionable water. Either of them can lead to gastrointestinal illness, such as vomiting or diarrhea. Other potential nasties include bacteria, such as salmonella or E. coli, and viruses including hepatitis A or enterovirus. Ingesting any of these will cause a bad day to get so much worse.

There are two types of methods for rendering water potable. Filtration is removing the microorganisms and other potentially harmful things from the water. Disinfection is killing or otherwise rendering inert the bad critters and such.

The first step, regardless of the method you choose, is to run the water through a coffee filter, clean T-shirt, or other material to remove as much sediment and debris as possible. This helps the filtration or disinfection method to work more efficiently.

This type of prefiltering will not make the water safe to drink, though. All it does is remove the big objects.

## FILTRATION

If your budget allows, a commercial filtration system is definitely the way to go. They work far better than any DIY solution. While there are dozens of different filters on the market, we're only looking at a few of them here. Each one has pros and cons.

### SAWYER MINI

This is a point-of-use filter, meaning it filters the water as you drink it. The use of the filter is simplicity itself. There is a straw you can dip into the water source, you can fill the included pouch, screw the filter onto any standard water or soda bottle, or attach it inline to most hydration packs.

The MINI is inexpensive. It is lightweight, topping the scales at a mere 2 ounces (55 g). It doesn't use any chemicals, so it doesn't impart any taste to the water it filters. It will remove 99.99999 percent of all waterborne bacteria, including those that cause E. coli. It will also remove 99.9999 percent of all waterborne protozoa, such as cryptosporidium and giardia. It will even remove all microplastics.

### GUARDIAN GRAVITY FILTER

As the name implies, this is a gravity-fed system. You first fill the 10-liter reservoir with water that you've sourced from the wild, and then hang it from a tree or hook. The water is filtered as it runs through the attached tube, removing sediment, microplastics, viruses, and other microorganisms, leaving you with clean water that's safe to drink.

The creators of this equipment state that it will remove 99.99 percent of viruses, 99.9 percent of protozoa, and 99.9999 percent of bacteria. There is also a two-stage charcoal filter that will improve the taste of the water. If you hang the unit about 6 feet (1.8 m) up, the resulting flow rate is about a liter every two minutes, meaning that this is an excellent choice if you have several water bottles you need to fill at a time.

### JUVO GROUP WATER FILTER

If you have the money to invest in it, this is an ideal filtration solution for a family or small group. It is the only pump-based filter on the short list here, and the mechanism is similar to a bicycle pump. You simply toss the intake tube into your water source, then pump the filter a few times before clear, clean water comes out.

in the water, but they just can't hurt you any longer.

### BOILING

This is probably the most fail-safe way to disinfect water. Any microscopic critters in the water that could harm you will be killed by the time water reaches boiling point. In fact, water doesn't even need to get to a rolling boil to be rendered safe. When water is brought to 150°F (65.5°C) and kept there for about 6 minutes, the water is considered pasteurized, which means all harmful microorganisms have been killed. The actual boiling point of water is 212°F (100°F). We often just say to bring water to a boil because that's a recognizable indicator it has been heated sufficiently.

The JUVO system will remove 99.9999 percent of bacteria and 99.99 percent of protozoa, as well as heavy metals, chemicals, sediments, and more. With its stainless steel construction, the filter system is durable and robust, easily up to any heavy-duty use. It is a pricey option, however, it will handle just about any water that you're likely to find.

If you invest in a handy gadget called a water pasteurization indicator, or WAPI, you can conserve fuel by heating water to a lower, but no less effective, temperature. A WAPI is simply a small tube with some wax inside. You suspend the WAPI in the water with the wax at the top of the tube. Once the wax has melted and gone to the bottom of the tube, the water is safe to use. The WAPI can be used over and over.

### DISINFECTION

Where filtration systems remove the harmful impurities in the water, disinfection renders them inert or otherwise harmless. They'll still be

Obviously, you'll want to let it cool for a while before drinking. Most people notice a flat taste to the water, too. This can be improved by either adding some kind of drink mix to it, such as Kool-Aid, or by pouring the water back and forth between a couple of clean containers. Doing so lets air back into the water.

The downside to this method is you can realistically only boil so much water at a time. The larger the container of water, the more fuel it will take to heat it up to at least 150°F (65.5°C), let alone all the way up to 212°F (100°F) for a rolling boil. It also takes time to heat the water and then let it cool down sufficiently to use.

## CHEMICAL TREATMENTS

There are many different brands of water purification tablets, including Micropur and Portable Aqua. Some utilize chlorine dioxide; others use a form of iodine. These all work well for short-term situations but aren't suited for the long haul. Once the bottle has been opened, the lifespan of the tablets is limited to about a year. Many, although certainly not all, types of tablets will impart a taste to the water that some find undesirable.

As many preppers and survivalists already know, nonscented chlorine bleach can be used to disinfect water. It doesn't take much. Just two drops per quart or eight drops per gallon (3.75 liters) will suffice. If the water is really cloudy, double the amount of bleach. Let the water sit for about 30 minutes, then sniff it. You should smell a slight chlorine odor. If not, do it all over again.

As with the water purification tablets, bleach has a limited shelf life. A bottle of bleach stored at room temperature, about 70°F (21°C), will remain viable for about a year. Something to keep in mind, is that it could have taken upward of a month or two for that bottle to get

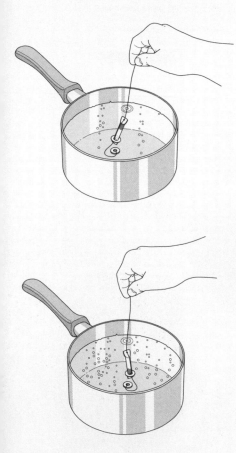

from the factory to the store. So, the 12-month shelf life is already down to maybe 10 months when you bring it home. If your home gets really warm, say 90°F (32°C), for long periods of time, that could shorten the shelf-life of your bottle of bleach down to three months or so. While it is great to have on hand, it just isn't going to last through a long-term disaster.

# POOL
## SHOCK

A kissing cousin to bleach is pool shock. Here's how to use it for water disinfection.

Purchase calcium hypochlorite, also known as pool shock, at any store that sells pool equipment. Given the proliferation of quick-set swimming pools in the last several years, you can probably find it just about anywhere in your area. Make sure you're buying the granular form, not the liquid. The percentage of calcium hypochlorite to inert ingredients will vary between products and brands. You want a minimum of 68% calcium hypochlorite. Be double-darn sure to read all of the warning labels too, particularly the ones that apply to storage requirements. As a general rule, it should be kept cool and dry and never in a metal container.

Add one teaspoon of shock to one gallon of water. An old bleach bottle is perfect for this, but any durable plastic bottle will suffice. Swirl and shake the bottle to thoroughly mix the water and

chemical. Be sure to prominently label this container and store it well away from pets and children.

This is added to your water in a ratio of 1 part chlorine solution to 100 parts water. I find it easiest to think of it in terms of ounces. One quart (which is roughly one liter) is 32 ounces. According to the formula, this means we need to add 0.32 ounce of chlorine solution. So, one-third of an ounce of solution per quart or liter of water.

A two-liter bottle is approximately one half-gallon or 2 quarts. This means you'd add about two-thirds of an ounce of the solution. Just like when using chlorine bleach for water disinfection, you should smell a faint whiff of chlorine from the water before drinking it.

You may notice the lack of exact measurements here. As a practical matter, precision isn't truly necessary for the disinfection to work. Even the Environmental Protection Agency (EPA) isn't exact with their measurements when talking about this practice.

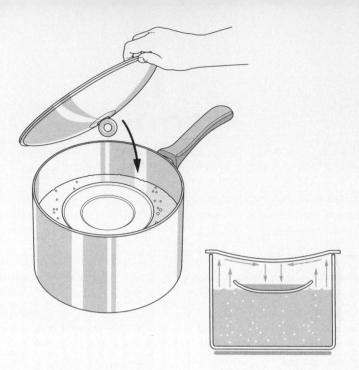

## DISTILLATION

There is one other method of water disinfection worth discussing. The technique involves boiling water to create steam, then collecting that steam and condensing it back into liquid water. The steam leaves behind all of the impurities and what condenses is pure water. Distillation is also the only method mentioned here that will turn saltwater into potable water.

There are several water distillers on the market today. One I particularly recommend is the Gravi-Stil manufactured and sold by SHTFandGo.com. It has the bonus of filtration in addition to distillation.

A simple DIY method requires a deep kettle, such as you'd use for making a large pot of soup, a matching lid, and a shallow glass dish that can easily fit into the kettle. The glass dish needs to be small enough to float. Plastic will not work, because it will warp under the heat you'll be using.

Fill the kettle about two-thirds with the dirty water. Float the glass dish in the water and put the kettle on the stove burner or campfire coals. Put the lid upside down on the kettle. The lid should be concave and the curve directed into the kettle. Heat the water just to the point that it starts to steam. Don't let it get to a full boil becuase it will sink your glass dish.

As the water steams, it will condense on the lid and then drip into the glass dish. This isn't a rapid process and it can take an hour or more for a good amount of water to collect in the dish. You can speed things up by adding ice or snow to the lid. The rapid temperature change as the steam hits the lid will increase the speed of the condensation.

Be sure to remove and empty the glass dish before it sinks to the bottom of the kettle and ends up with dirty water overflowing into the dish.

Commercial water distillers will work faster and provide more water than this DIY method, but when Amazon isn't making deliveries because the world came to an end, you can probably scrounge these supplies fairly easily.

## WATER IS LIFE
Water is vital, now and especially when the faucets stop running. Get a step ahead by not only storing water but also the supplies and equipment necessary to provide clean water when you'll need it most.

# CHAPTER 2
# FOOD

OTHER THAN PERHAPS WATER, FOOD IS AT THE TOP OF THE LIST WHEN MOST PEOPLE THINK ABOUT WHAT TO STORE IN CASE OF AN EMERGENCY. NOBODY WANTS TO GO TO BED HUNGRY IF IT CAN BE AVOIDED. WITH THE POSSIBLE EXCEPTION OF DEFENSE WEAPONS AND AMMUNITION, FOOD WILL PROBABLY BE YOUR LARGEST EXPENSE WHEN IT COMES TO EMERGENCY PREPAREDNESS.

## TYPES OF FOOD TO STORE

Sometimes the first instinct is to run out and order a pallet or two of specially packaged survival food, but that's one of the worst things you can do. Not only is that method prohibitively expensive for most people, there's usually little actual food in those products. Fortunately, there are several other options.

## GROCERY STORE

As a practical matter, just about anything you'll need for a comprehensive food storage program can be found in an average supermarket. Some things might be priced just a hair more than you'd pay at a warehouse store or another outlet, but if you factor in travel time, gasoline, and membership fees, you'll probably break even.

Here are just a few examples of food you'll find at the grocery store that will store well long-term:

- White rice
- Dried beans
- Canned goods
- Split peas
- Dry pasta
- Pasta sauce
- Pouch meats (chicken, tuna)
- Soup mix
- Instant mashed potatoes
- Flour
- Sugar
- Baking mix

# FOREVER
## FOODS

While they won't form a complete diet, there are several foods that will last nearly forever, if stored properly. Keep them cool, dry, and away from sunlight and they'll be good for decades.

**HONEY:** If it crystalizes, put the container in a saucepan of warm water for a while and it'll melt.

**SALT:** Salt can have added iodine, which is good for our thyroids but bad for long-term storage. Opt for non-iodized salt for the pantry.

**WHITE RICE:** Store it in an airtight container. Note that brown rice has oil in the hull that will turn rancid over time. This is why white rice is specified.

**SUGAR:** If it gets damp, it'll harden into a rock, so take extra precautions to keep it humidity-free by sealing it well.

**CANNED GOODS:** Okay, these won't remain good forever, but they'll last many years if you store them away from moisture and heat. If they develop a bulge, trash them.

For anything that requires more than just heating, read the instructions to ensure you'll have all you need to prepare it properly.

## HOME PRESERVED

While there is a learning curve when it comes to canning and dehydrating, preservation skills are important to master. They will allow you to take better advantage of sales, where you can pick up extra produce or meat at a great price and preserve at home for storage.

Another distinct benefit to preserving food at home is that you're certain exactly what's in it. You control the amount of sodium or salt, sugar, and other ingredients. The downside is that full canning jars are fragile, heavy, and not easily transported, if the need arises.

## MILITARY RATIONS

Often called MREs, which stands for Meals, Ready to Eat, these are a popular choice for preppers and survivalists. A full and complete MRE contains an entrée, a side dish, a cracker or bread with spread, dessert, and a beverage mix. These items along with utensils, condiments, and a flameless heater are all contained in a large sealed pouch.

Entrée options include beef stew, chicken gumbo, pasta marinara, and even vegetarian chili.

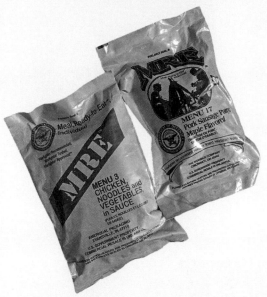

MREs are nice to have because they are calorie-dense and some of them are even pretty tasty. Plus, they are completely cooked and require nothing more than reheating, although in a pinch they can be eaten cold. However, they are pricey when compared to other options. They are also decidedly heavy and bulky, but these problems can be mitigated to a degree by opening the pouch and distributing the contents as you see fit.

One last thing about MREs. They are notorious for causing constipation. While in the short-term that means you'll cut down on your daily use of toilet paper, looking ahead to when your body finally lets loose, let's just say that you'll be thankful if the toilet is working by that time.

## CAMP FOOD

Stop at any sporting goods store and you'll find a variety of freeze-dried or dehydrated food pouches from brands like Wise or Mountain House. These require nothing more than hot water to rehydrate for eating and are usually prepared right in the pouch.

These meals are convenient and very lightweight. They can be a little expensive but buying them in bulk can cut the individual cost a little. The downside with them is that many varieties are high in sodium, which can be problematic for those on restricted diets. One outdoor survival instructor I know has mentioned that if he eats these for more than a few days in a row, he notices a distinct swelling in his hands and fingers, due to the sodium content.

## PRODUCING FOOD AT HOME

There are many foods that can be grown at home, even if your space is severely limited. You might not be able to produce everything you'll need, but anything you can grow yourself decreases the amount you'll need to purchase elsewhere. I firmly believe that virtually everyone can grow something, regardless of where they live.

### CONTAINER GARDENING

The idea here is simple. Instead of digging up a patch of the backyard, tilling the soil, and planting rows of crops, you just grow your plants in pots on the patio, deck, or even driveway. This is an excellent option for those who live in areas governed by associations that forbid traditional gardens, as well as those who lack any kind of actual yard space. Tomatoes, potatoes, green beans, peas, and more can all be grown in pots, although some may require a trellis or fence to climb.

### RAISED BEDS

This is kind of a combination of traditional gardening and using containers. Instead of pots scattered here and there, garden beds are built using lumber. The beds are filled with prepared soil and

# ✕ COMFORT FOODS

Don't overlook the value of having foods in your stash that serve little purpose beyond just tasting good or having sentimental value. Anything you can do to calm nerves and improve morale during a crisis is beneficial. While the preferred choices will differ from one person to the next, some of the more common comfort foods include:

- Chicken noodle soup

- Mashed potatoes

- Chocolate

- Biscuits and gravy

- Chocolate chip cookies

- Macaroni and cheese

- Popcorn

- Pancake mix

- Brownie mix

- Hot chocolate mix

then seeds or seedlings are planted. Mel Bartholomew may not have invented it, but he sure popularized it with his Square Foot Gardening concept. These do require a little yard space, but it is an intensive approach that can grow a lot of food in a small area.

## VERTICAL GARDENING

If you have a fence, this might be a good approach to try. The basic idea is to attach plastic rain gutters in rows along a section of fence, with the gutters sealed off at each end. You then fill them with soil and plant your seeds in them. Strawberries, various greens, pole beans, and more will do well with this method.

## EDIBLE LANDSCAPING

Many homes, even in dense urban areas, have flowerbeds. Replace them with food-bearing plants. Some great options for this include peppers and eggplants, as well as any number of herbs. There are even several types of edible flowers, such as rose, lavender, and fennel. Alternatively, you could leave the decorative plants and just scatter in some edibles, such as onions and garlic interspersed throughout the flowerbed. This approach is another good option for those who live in strict HOA [homeowner association] communities where the bylaws prohibit actual gardens. Few nongardeners will recognize garlic, potatoes, carrots, and similar crops by the parts that are visible above the dirt.

## PRESERVATION METHODS

Over the centuries that humankind has been hunting, foraging, and growing food, we've developed several ways to keep the bounty edible for long periods of time.

### DEHYDRATION

By removing most of the moisture from food, mold, bacteria, and other nastiness won't grow and spoil it. People have been doing this since before recorded history, preserving everything from vegetables to meat. The easiest approach today is to use a store-bought dehydrator like the one shown below. It will let you to control the temperature and fan speed, so you are in better control of the final product. Some foods, such as jerky or fruit, can be eaten as is, while others, such as vegetables or potato flakes, will need to be rehydrated.

The general rule of thumb is to slice the food to about ¼ inch (5 mm) thick and make the pieces as uniform as possible, so they dry evenly. Flip the pieces every so often during the drying process. The "doneness" varies by the food, but you're looking for it to be dry, not sticky or moist.

In a pinch, you can dehydrate food in your oven. Set the temperature to 120°F (50°C). If it won't go that low, set it to "warm". Another option, in warm weather at least, is to use your car. Set trays of sliced food in the rear window or on the dash and cover them lightly with thin cloths to keep bugs away. Crack the windows an inch or two so that moisture can escape.

### CANNING

There are two type of home canning—water bath and pressure. While there are some similarities, it is important to use the proper method for the type of food you're preserving in jars (despite the term "canning"). Otherwise, you could be risking botulism or other problems.

Water bath canning involves completely immersing sealed jars of food into boiling water for a prescribed amount of time. This method of canning is suitable for acidic foods, such as fruits, jam, salsa, and pickles. You can find books or look online for complete

information on canning, but here we describe some of the differences.

Pressure canning is a little more involved. First, you'll need a pressure canner. It is important to understand that a pressure cooker and a pressure canner are not necessarily the same thing.

While some models of cookers can double as canners, not all of them are suitable, so be sure to read the box and check with the manufacturer. In this method, the jars of food are placed inside the canner and "processed," or kept at a specific pressure, for a specified length of time. This method

# DEHYDRATION
## VS. FREEZE-DRYING

Costs aside, there are a few practical differences between these two methods of preservation, and these apply to store-bought products as well as those you can produce at home.

**STORAGE LIFE:** Dehydrated foods will still retain about 20 percent of their original moisture content and therefore tend to remain viable for a few years before degradation can happen. Freeze drying removes upward of 98 percent of the moisture, which means the food will last a couple of decades or more.

**REHYDRATION:** Dehydrated foods tend to take a little longer to reconstitute and often need hot water to do so effectively. Freeze-dried foods rehydrate quicker and will do so with hot or cold water.

**TASTE/TEXTURE:** Dehydrated foods are sometimes a little chewier than their freeze-dried counterparts, because the dehydration process actually cooks the food a little as it dries. Freeze dried food will usually turn out nearly the same texture and taste that it had before it was dried.

**NUTRITION:** The dehydration process can reduce the nutritional components of food by almost half, while freeze-drying keeps them largely intact.

While it certainly seems that freeze-drying is the better option, you have to weigh the costs of the food products, and the equipment needed to process it at home.

of canning is used for low-acid foods, such as meats and most vegetables.

## FREEZE-DRYING

Until recently, this type of food preservation wasn't really viable at home, because it requires specialized equipment. A few years ago, Harvest Right came out with a line of benchtop units that can be used in the home. They are pricey, with even the smallest one costing a few thousand dollars. But, if you're looking to preserve large quantities of food, or you're working with a small group of families, it might be worth the investment

Freeze drying is similar to dehydration in that the goal is to remove moisture from the food. However, where a dehydrator works by heating the food to increase evaporation, a freeze-dryer will first freeze the food, then reduce the pressure while increasing the temperature, causing the frozen water in the food to convert directly to vapor, a process called sublimation. The end result is perfectly preserved food that rehydrates easily.

## CALCULATING FOOD NEEDS

One of the most common questions people face when starting to put together their food-storage plan is determining how much they need to have available at home. Obviously, this will be different for everyone. A family of five will need exponentially more food than a single person who lives alone.

There is no easy way to calculate this, but one of the simplest is to create a menu plan and use it as a guideline. Grab pen and paper and plot out meals for a full two weeks. Include breakfast, lunch, dinner, snacks – don't leave anything out. For each meal, list everything you'll need for it. As you go through this, concentrate on listing foods and ingredients that you know will store for a reasonable length of time.

It sounds a little monotonous, but when you think about it, many families already have a basic routine, at least for dinner. In my house, we have Meatless Monday and Taco Tuesday, for example, and I know we're not alone with that sort of routine.

# THE TRUTH
## ABOUT
## EXPIRATION DATES

We've all been there. Standing at the kitchen counter, looking at a can of soup that we just found at the back of the cabinet and upon seeing it is three months past expiration, wondering if it might still be safe to eat.

Here's the deal. Expiration dates aren't really an accurate measure of whether the food inside the package has spoiled. Instead, it is merely the last date that the manufacturer will guarantee the best taste/quality and the nutritional value noted on the label.

Just because that soup is a few months older than the date printed doesn't mean it will make you sick if you eat it. That said, the further away you are from that date, the greater the chance that the contents will not be palatable.

Once you have the meal plan worked out for 14 days, it is simple math to create one for a month, two months, or more. Toss in a few extra meals for some added variety, if you'd like.

This isn't a bulletproof plan, but it will get you moving in the right direction. My suggestion is to set two weeks as your first goal, then expand from there until you're comfortable with the amount of food you keep in the house. The important thing to remember is that empty calories aren't going to get you far in the long run. You need to ensure you're storing real food with actual nutrition.

## ROTATION

One of the biggest mistakes you can make, when it comes to a food storage plan, is to buy it and forget it. While there are many products that are specifically designed to have long-term shelf lives, a better approach is to use your food and replace it as you go along. Doing so ensures you always have the absolute freshest possible products on hand at any given time.

### STORE WHAT YOU EAT

Don't drop a ton of money buying food products you've never eaten before, just for the sake of having something on the shelves. The aftermath of a major crisis

is the wrong time to find out you're allergic to some obscure ingredient or to learn that your digestive system really doesn't like a particular brand of food. If you want to expand your range of food choices, you can buy a small amount as a sample and see if it agrees with you. If it does, then invest in a larger order.

### EAT WHAT YOU STORE

First in, first out is the name of the game. Also known by the acronym FIFO, this is the heart of a rotation plan. As you store your food, always put the newest items toward the back and keep the oldest at the front of the shelf. The goal is to use your food before it goes bad. This approach also goes a long way toward ensuring you're only storing food that you know your family will eat, even in austere conditions.

## STORAGE CONSIDERATIONS

There are only a few people who have massive amounts of space in which they can store any manner of food and other supplies. In fact, for most of us, our storage space is limited, and most of it is already claimed. However, there may still be some options available.

The basic requirements for food storage are cool, dark, and dry. This eliminates attics, garages, and outbuildings that aren't climate controlled. The basement can work if it isn't damp and doesn't flood. But for many people the best options will be in the main living areas of the home.

If space is an issue, here are some other options to consider:

UNDER BEDS: Purchase plastic totes that will easily slide on the floor and fill them with canned goods and similar items.

CLOSETS: There is often unused space on the floor against the back wall. You might be able to rearrange some of the clothing that's already there and make some extra room. While you're in there, take a look at the interior wall above the door. Often, there's enough space there to hang a shelf or two. Those shelves won't hold a ton of food, but every little bit helps.

EXTRA SHELVING: Depending on the layout of your home and how the space is already being used, you might be able to run shelving around the perimeter of a bedroom or home office up near the ceiling. We did this along one wall of our kitchen and added more than 15 square feet (1.4 m²) of storage space that works great for pasta and other dry goods.

HIDING IN PLAIN SIGHT: If you take a couple of totes, stack them together, and drape them with a nice tablecloth or similar fabric, you've just made a nifty end table.

When you're scattering your food throughout the home, it is a good idea to keep track of what you have, where it is, what you use, and what you need to replenish. Until you get into the habit of doing this, it will indeed seem like a giant inconvenience. But, after just a little time, you'll start to see the beauty of it. You'll know at a glance what is on the shelves and where the holes are that need to be filled. For many, a simple handwritten notebook will suffice. Others prefer a more high-tech approach with spreadsheets or one of the many apps that are available on the market. Find what works for you and stick with it.

## ORDER OF CONSUMPTION

In order to make the best and most efficient use of your food stores, it is important not to dig into the long-term storage immediately when a disaster happens. Instead, take a more methodical approach to avoid wasting resources.

Most households have food in the refrigerator and freezer. If you lose power, do what you can to use it before it goes bad. According to the United States Department of Agriculture (USDA), food that's kept in the refrigerator will stay safe for about four hours, provided you don't open the door over and over. Any milk, cooked pasta, meat, and raw eggs should be tossed after spending more than 2 hours above 40°F (4°C).

For the freezer, you should have about 24 hours before things start to melt. As a general guideline, if food items are cold to the touch and there are still some ice crystals present, the food should be safe to either refreeze or cook.

With those guidelines in mind, see about working your way through what's in the refrigerator before digging into the deep storage. Sure, this might make for a couple of pretty weird meals, but at least it won't all just go into the trash. If you're looking at a fairly large quantity of food, consider inviting over a neighbor or two for a feast.

If it appears that the crisis will probably last more than a day, whatever you won't be able to cook and consume before it goes bad should be preserved in some way, if possible. This could mean dehydration, pressure canning, water bath canning, or another method.

Of course, nobody is saying you can't mix and match. Feel free to cook up some rice to go along with the thawed pork chops and the fresh green beans from the vegetable drawer in the refrigerator. But, do what you can to make

# TRAVEL
## TIP

If you're heading out of town for a day or more, fill a coffee cup about halfway with water and freeze it. Then, place a penny on top of the ice in the cup and put it back in the freezer. When you get home, check the cup. If the penny is at the bottom, you'll know you lost power for a long enough period of time that the food in the freezer should probably be tossed.

the best use of what you have available.

## OFF-GRID COOKING

If the power is out, a gas stove can still usually be lit with a match. However, if your appliances are electric, you will need to rely on other ways to heat food and water. Plan ahead so you have multiple options available.

### GRILLS

Even urban residents often have a gas grill on the patio or balcony. These can be used to prepare more than just burgers and hot dogs. Pick up an extra tank of fuel to keep on hand, so you don't run out at the worst possible time. A charcoal grill is also useful, but they tend to be less efficient for heating water and soups, simply due to the amount of fuel used. Be as efficient as you can and do double or triple duty when you fire up the grill by, for example, heating water for washing while you're also cooking dinner. If you run out of charcoal, you can use sticks and twigs.

### CAMP STOVE

Tabletop versions will be about as close to cooking on your normal stovetop as you can get. There are other models that are just single burners that screw on to the fuel canister. Those are mostly used for heating water for rehydrating freeze-dried food. There are also small alcohol stoves that work well for heating water or small saucepans of soup or stew. Still others use biomass such as twigs, instead of pressurized gas or liquid fuels. No matter which option you choose, make sure you stock up on plenty of fuel for it.

## GEL FUEL
Sometimes just referred to by the brand name Sterno, these little cans are often used by restaurants and catering services to keep food warm. The key word there is "warm." A can won't provide enough heat to actually cook anything or even bring water to a boil. But, given a little time, it will heat up a can of soup enough to make it a little more enticing.

## CAMPFIRE
If you have a yard, you might be able to build a campfire. A similar option is the ubiquitous patio fire pit. However, cooking over an open fire is almost as much art as it is skill and requires a fair amount of practice to get right. Start now with having small cookouts in the backyard. If you want to rely on this option, you should also see what you can do about stocking up on a supply of dry firewood. Do not store it next to your house, because insects might travel from the wood to your home. Find a spot somewhere else in the yard that you can use.

## SOLAR OVEN
These are easy to make at home, but they work slowly. The basic principle is that solar radiation enters the oven through a clear lid and it is then directed at the cooking vessel via foil that lines the inside of the oven. Over time, the vessel heats up and cooks the food. This usually takes hours, so this isn't an option for a quick snack. Instead, you'll start dinner cooking around mid-morning.

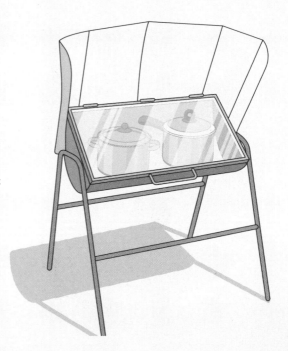

## KITCHEN ODDS AND ENDS

There are a few nonfood items that you might consider picking up and storing, just in case.

A manual can opener will be necessary to access a fair amount of the food you've stored. Pick up a few, so that you have a backup in case one breaks or gets lost. Keep one in a kitchen drawer and another stashed with your canned goods.

Depending upon the nature of the emergency, you might not have easy access to water to wash dishes. A pack of paper plates and bowls could come in handy in those situations. After use, they can be tossed in the trash or burned in the backyard. Silverware takes little water to wash, however, disposable plastic utensils might still be good to have on hand.

# WONDERBAG

Working something like a slow cooker, the Wonderbag is a kind of insulated sack. You bring your food to a boil, then place the covered pot into the Wonderbag. It stays hot for hours, slowly simmering until you're ready to eat. It will help you to conserve fuel because you don't need to keep the pot boiling. Find it at WonderbagWorld.com.

Many average pots and pans won't do well when subjected to the high heat of a campfire or a patio grill. They could warp and any plastic handles could melt. Camp cookware isn't too expensive, especially if you can find a set at a rummage sale or thrift shop. Of course, the ideal is to use cast iron both in and out of the kitchen, but that's not always practical for everyone.

A French press, or cafetiere, lets you enjoy your morning cup of java, no matter what's going on around you. They aren't expensive, but many are somewhat fragile, so you might want to pick up a couple in case one breaks. Another option is an old-fashioned percolator, the type that can be used over an open flame like a campfire.

## GO SLOW

Most people will not be able to put together a comprehensive food storage program overnight. Doing so would be extremely expensive and require an awful lot of work, which in turn would probably lead to frustration and abandonment of the whole enterprise.

A better approach is to do the work in small chunks. Each time you go to the store, toss one or two extra things into your cart and add them to your pantry or other storage. It won't take long before you start to see your stockpile growing.

You can use coupons when they will get you a better deal than store brands and always shop in sales. Shop smart and you'll be eating tomorrow at today's prices.

# CHAPTER 3
# SHELTER

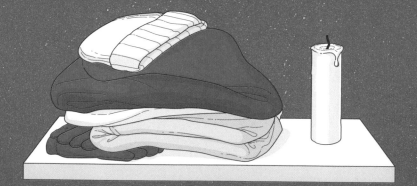

**ONE OF OUR BASIC SURVIVAL NEEDS IS PROTECTION FROM THE ELEMENTS. IN THE GRAND SCHEME OF THINGS, WE'RE PERHAPS NOT AS DURABLE AS WE'D LIKE TO THINK. IF WE GET TOO COLD OR TOO WARM, IT CAN QUITE LITERALLY KILL US AND, IN MANY CASES, IT'LL HAPPEN FASTER THAN WE MIGHT EXPECT.**

When we talk about shelter, we're talking about being able to stay out of the weather, such as snow and rain. In addition, we're referring to some kind of temperature control. We need to be able to keep our bodies within a fairly narrow range of temperature to survive, about 97°F to 99°F (36–37°C). If you get too hot, you could end up hyperthermic. Too cold, hypothermic. Either direction is bad news.

Once upon a time, homes were built with features meant to naturally heat or cool them, such as high ceilings to trap warm air up away from us in the summer and smaller rooms that were easier to keep warm in the winter. Unfortunately, most homes in urban areas, especially apartments and condominiums, are built for powered climate control, with air-conditioning and heaters of some type. As a result, if there is a power outage, it can suddenly be an issue

trying to keep your body in that ideal temperature range.

In addition to the physical problems that extreme temperatures can inflict, there's a psychological element at work as well. Having the means to get ourselves to a more comfortable temperature helps improve our morale and will certainly free up our mind to tackle other problems we're facing.

An advantage the city dweller has over their country cousins is that if you're too hot or too cold at home, you can usually go somewhere else that's more comfortable. For example, during heat waves, many cities will set up designated cooling stations, typically at public libraries and similar locations, where members of the public are welcome to hang out and get out of the heat. However, you should plan ahead and have alternate means of heating and cooling your home, just in case.

## HANDLING HOT TEMPERATURES

When the summer heats up, that's when we start seeing brownouts (for example, when the electricity supply voltage dips and your lights dim for a bit) and rolling blackouts hitting urban areas. Everyone is cranking up their air-conditioning and the utility companies can't entirely keep up with the demand. For most people, this is an inconvenience, but for some, it can be truly life threatening.

### HEAT-RELATED ILLNESSES

While few people enjoy being hot and sweaty for long periods of time, there are real and dangerous health concerns when it comes to getting notably overheated. The two major ones are heat exhaustion and heat stroke. It is important to be able to recognize the symptoms so you can take action immediately if you observe them.

### HEAT EXHAUSTION

When your body loses an excessive amount of salt and water, heat exhaustion is the result. Symptoms include:

- Cold, clammy skin

- Fast but weak pulse

- Weakness

- Headache

- Nausea/vomiting

- Fainting

- Elevated body temperature

Treatment for heat exhaustion at home includes using cool compresses on the neck, wrists, and head. A cool, not cold, bath can also help. Otherwise, loosen clothing and get the person to a cooler environment, such as in the shade or somewhere with a breeze. Frequent sips of water will also help, but don't let the person gulp it. If you do, he or she will probably vomit, which will only exacerbate the situation.

## HEAT STROKE

If heat exhaustion is left untreated, it can lead to heat stroke, which in turn can be deadly. At this stage, the body loses the ability to regulate its temperature. It is therefore imperative to externally lower the core temperature quickly, but carefully. Symptoms of heat stroke include:

- Body temperature of 103°F (39.4°F) or higher

- Confusion

- Slurred speech

- Dizziness

- Headache

- Hot, dry skin

- Passing out

To treat heat stroke, you need to cool down the afflicted person as fast as possible. If emergency medical services are available, call them. If you have to handle things on your own, an ice bath is an excellent option, if feasible. Failing that, go with cool, damp towels at pulse points, such as the inner wrists and sides of the neck. If an electric fan isn't available, do what you can to manually fan the air around them to facilitate further cooling.

## COOLING STRATEGIES

There are several ways you can combat heat. Try a combination of approaches until you find ones that work well in your situation.

### STAY LOW

If you can, get as low to the ground as possible. If you live in a two-story home, stay downstairs. A basement is even better, if that's an option. Warm air rises (that's basic physics), so the lower you can get, relatively speaking, the cooler you'll be.

### AIR MOVEMENT

Evaporation is a cooling process, which is why we sweat, and you can speed it along by getting the air moving around you. Have a few battery-operated fans squirreled away, along with batteries for them, so you can break them out when the temperature skyrockets. Even a handheld paper fan is better than nothing. You could also open windows to get cross-ventilation going throughout the home. Any movement of the air will help.

## ADD WATER

Taking a cool shower can help a lot, at least temporarily. Don't, however, make it too cold. Our bodies are built in a funny kind of way and if you get too cold in the shower, your body will work to increase your internal temperature, which will defeat the purpose of cooling down in the first place.

You can add moist towels to your wrists or the sides of your neck. The evaporation on the skin where the blood vessels are closest to the surface will help. A mister bottle can also be beneficial. Spray your face and neck periodically to let the water evaporate.

## CLOSE OFF HOT ROOMS

Rooms that have big windows tend to heat up fast. Close the doors to them and keep them closed. You might go so far as to put rolled up towels at the bottom to keep out as much of that hot air as possible.

## BUILD A SWAMP COOLER

This is a simple DIY project that requires a small, battery-operated fan, a Styrofoam cooler, and some ice. When shopping for the cooler, bigger is better, so get the largest one you can find.

STEP 1: Cut a hole in the cooler lid that's just big enough to fit the fan snugly. Figure about an inch (2.5 cm) less in diameter than the fan itself and keep in mind that you'll be inserting the fan so it blows into the cooler. Put the hole toward one end of the lid, not just in the center.

STEP2: On the side of the cooler away from where the hole in the lid is located, cut three or four smaller holes a few inches from the bottom. Put them in a square or diamond shape and have them roughly equal to the size of the fan hole in total. So, for example, if the fan is about four inches (10 cm) across, each of the four holes should be about an inch.

STEP 3: Fill the bottom of the cooler with ice, up to where those smaller holes are located. Put on the cooler lid, insert the fan, and turn it on. If needed, you can secure the fan in place using duct tape. Cold air will be coming out from the side holes.

This project works best with solid blocks of ice, instead of ice cubes.

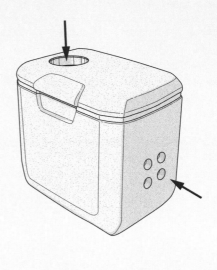

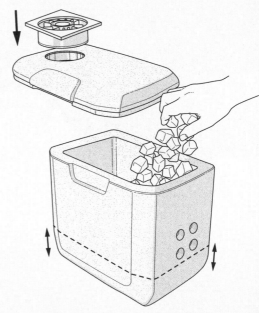

Plan ahead by purchasing the cooler and building the unit, along with keeping ice in the freezer.

One option for the latter is to fill several empty and clean 2-liter soda bottles with water and freeze them. Leave an inch or two (2.5–5 cm) of headspace to allow for ice expansion. Then, you can just lay the frozen bottles down in the cooler when you run the fan. Plus, this will give you some extra potable water already stored, which is always a plus.

## HANDLING COLD TEMPERATURES

There are many reasons why you might need to work out how to stay warm, even in your own home. Let's say you live in a climate where the temperatures dip to freezing or below in the winter, and your furnace goes out. Or you live in an area where it doesn't typically get that cold, but then it does and the power goes out due to the sudden high demand in the community.

## COLD-RELATED ILLNESSES

When the mercury plummets, there are a couple of major hazards to your health: frostbite and hypothermia. Both are dangerous, but both can be handled at home, at least to a certain point, if you know what to do.

## FROSTBITE

This occurs when skin and underlying tissue freeze. It typically affects appendages, such as fingers or toes, although it can happen to any skin that's exposed to the cold. If it isn't handled promptly, it can lead to severe damage, even amputation. Symptoms of frostbite include:

- Numbness

- Tingling

- Aching

- Discolored skin, either waxy and pale or turning blue

- Hardened areas of skin

Because ice crystals are forming within the tissue, it is important to handle any affected areas with the utmost care. Do not walk when you have frostbitten toes or feet and never rub the skin to try to warm it. If feasible, immerse the injured area in warm water. It should not be scalding hot. Otherwise, use body heat, such as by putting cold fingers under the armpit or between the legs. Seek medical attention if possible.

## HYPOTHERMIA

In this condition, your body temperature falls too low. Basically, when experiencing hypothermia from it you can't generate more heat than you're losing, so your core temperature drops. If it goes too low, you'll experience a variety of negative effects. What's worse, because hypothermia dramatically impacts your thinking and reasoning abilities, you may be unable to help yourself. The symptoms of hypothermia include:

- Fatigue

- Shivering

- Confusion and stumbling

As the condition worsens:

- Shivering stops

- Slowed pulse

- Dilated pupils

- Loss of consciousness

For treatment, getting the person warm is critical. If their clothing is wet, get it off and dry them as best you can. Then, warm them up, starting with the torso, using warm blankets or even body heat. You can also try warm drinks, but avoid alcohol.

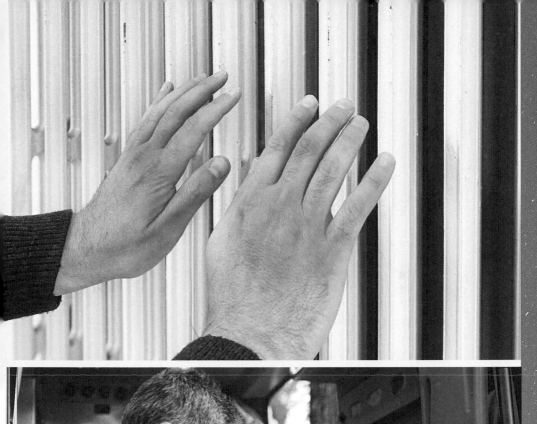
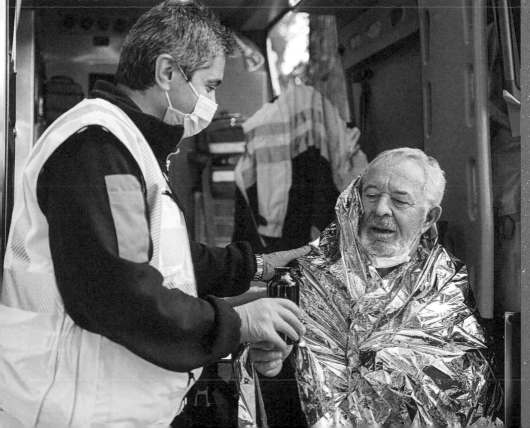

## WARMING STRATEGIES

Modern fireplaces don't generate that much heat for the home, with most of it going right up the chimney. And let's face it, there aren't that many apartments or condos equipped with wood-burning fireplaces anyway. So, how can you keep you and your family from freezing all night long? If you're unable or unwilling to seek shelter elsewhere, such as a local motel, there are some solutions you can try.

### CREATE A MINI SHELTER

One of the easiest things you can do is create a confined area within the home where everyone gathers.

The smaller the room, the better, but you probably don't want to do this in a bathroom, just for the sake of comfort. Choose the smallest bedroom instead. Hang blankets over the door and windows to reduce drafts. Depending on the size of the room and the number of family members, body heat alone should help to warm the room.

You can go a step further and set up a small tent in the room and herd everyone in there. Make a game of it with young children and pretend you're camping. Again, you're relying on body heat to warm up the space inside the tent. You can drape a blanket over the tent to

# LAYERS
## ARE IMPORTANT

When it comes to dressing for warmth, don't just rely on one heavy parka to get the job done. You're far better off wearing layers for a couple of reasons. The way it works is your body heat warms the air pockets between the layers of clothing, insulating you from the colder air around you. Plus, if you get too warm, you can remove a layer or two until you're comfortable. Then, as you cool off, you can put the layers back on.

Generally speaking, there are three layers: base, mid, and outer.

**BASE:** The clothing that you put on first and that touches your skin is the base layer. When dressing for warmth, it should be a wicking material, something that will move your sweat away from the body so it doesn't cool and chill you. Examples include polyester, nylon, and merino wool.

**MID:** An insulating layer, for example, a puffy-type jacket or a thick, warm shirt works as a mid layer. Down is a great material for this layer, as is wool.

**OUTER:** The primary purpose here is to shed water, such as rain and snow, as well as provide wind resistance. One of the key factors I look for with outerwear is breathability. You don't want something that is so watertight that you roast inside of it.

help keep more heat in. Along those same lines, if you don't have a tent try making an old-fashioned blanket fort like you did as a child. It might not be perfect, but anything you can do to trap body heat will help.

## INDOOR KEROSENE HEATER

These work very well, with a couple of caveats. For starters, you'll need to buy one and fuel for it ahead of the crisis. The chances are that if you wait until the emergency happens, you'll either not be able to get out to a store or, if you do manage to make your way there, you'll find they're sold out.

Make absolutely certain that the heater you purchase is designed for use indoors. The fumes will be minimal and there's less risk of carbon monoxide poisoning. Even so, you're best off setting it up near a window you can crack open. Not only will this help ventilate the room, it will reduce the odor of the kerosene.

## CANDLES

As anyone who has done the romantic, 'fill the room with lit candles' routine knows, there's a good amount of heat given off by them. However, that warmth comes at a price — danger. Open flames can certainly warm the room. They can also set the room on fire and give you a whole new set of problems to solve.

If you're going to resort to using candles for heat, go about it intelligently. Use heat-resistant surfaces for them to sit on and limit it to just one or two candles in a given area, closely monitored by someone responsible.

# CLAY POT
## HEATER

For the last few years, there's been a DIY heater project floating around on social media that involves using a few clay or terra-cotta pots and tea lights (small candles). Claims of being able to heat entire rooms with this setup abound.

The reality is that these homemade heaters can work, but in a limited space. The basic setup is to use a terra-cotta pot that's about 4 inches (10 cm) or so across at the top. Grab four tea lights and put them in a 2 x 2-inch (5 x 5-cm) square on a heatproof surface, such as a ceramic tile or even a cutting board. Turn the pot upside down and place it over the candles. Use small bricks or some other heat-resistant objects to raise the pot up a few inches so there's air circulation to the candles.

Within a short time, the pot will warm from the heat of the candles, which in turn will give off heat to the immediate area. It works, but it will never heat an entire room.

A couple warnings about this DIY project. First, any open flame is extremely dangerous. Every year, fire departments are called to homes that have caught fire because the residents were trying to use some type of alternative heat source, typically involving candles or other open flames.

On top of that, paraffin has a flash point of about 400°F (200°C). This means if the temperature inside your DIY heater gets high enough, those candles could burst into flames and cause some serious issues, including burning those sitting nearby.

**X** *Extreme* caution is advised.

# CHAPTER 4
# MEDICAL & HYGIENE

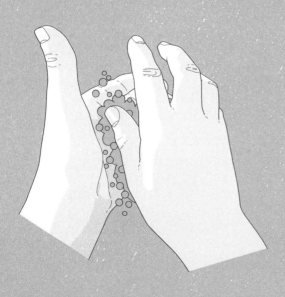

**THIS TENDS TO BE AN AREA WHERE MANY FAMILIES ARE DECIDEDLY UNPREPARED, OR AT LEAST UNDERPREPARED. SURE, YOU MIGHT HAVE A FIRST AID KIT, AND YOU MIGHT EVEN KNOW WHERE TO FIND IT IN A HURRY. BUT DO YOU KNOW WHAT'S INSIDE AND DO YOU KNOW HOW TO USE EACH OF THE COMPONENTS? AND WOULD IT BE ENOUGH TO HANDLE ANY SERIOUS INJURIES OR ILLNESSES THAT OCCUR IN THE WAKE OF A DISASTER?**

## TRAINING

The importance of having proper training in rendering first aid cannot be overstated. Knowing exactly how to handle common injuries not only allows you to take care of problems, it provides you with a degree of self-confidence that is crucial to have in an emergency.

It is well beyond the scope of this book to even begin to educate you on how to provide competent treatment to an injured person. It isn't something that can be properly addressed in just a few pages. However, there are several options available for this kind of education and training.

Start by inquiring with the Red Cross or similar agencies in your area. They may have classes scheduled and it is just a matter of signing up. If they don't, ask how to go about requesting a class be held.

Another route is to contact your fire department and see if they sponsor any training sessions. If they don't, they might be able to direct you to a person or agency that does.

Here is just one real-world example. On November 21, 2021, a Christmas parade in Waukesha, Wisconsin, was the site of tragedy.

An SUV sped through part of the parade route, striking numerous people. More than 50 individuals were injured and, while there were several fatalities, many of those hurt were saved by the rapid actions of both law enforcement and civilians trained in first aid. In particular, the quick application of tourniquets, along with other measures that were taken to stop blood loss, was credited with saving lives and limbs.

This event highlights the need for the general population to have basic medical training as well as to routinely carry of first aid supplies such as tourniquets.

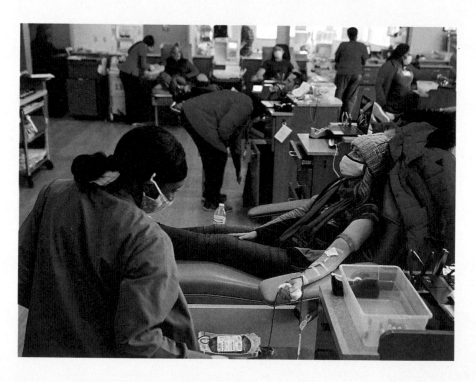

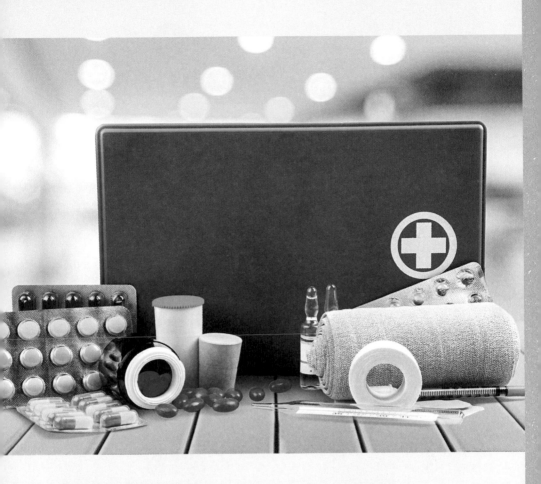

## FIRST AID KIT

Far too many people pick up a cheap first aid kit at a big box store, toss it into the bathroom cabinet, and call it a day. While that might suffice for the kinds of scrapes that happen while doing yard work, or perhaps a slight burn from grabbing the wrong end of a saucepan while cooking dinner, these kits are usually ridiculously lean on the supplies you really need.

Rest assured, I'm not suggesting every home invest in a complete surgical suite. However, if you're unable to easily reach out for medical help from the professionals, you should have more on hand than three adhesive bandages and a half used tube of ointment that expired a decade ago.

Also, keep in mind that while we're calling it a kit, it need not be confined to a single container on a shelf. In fact, if you're diligent about your medical preps, it won't all fit nicely into a shoebox or something similar. While the bathroom or hall closet might be a common choice for storing them, these areas aren't set in stone. Keep these items where it makes sense to do so in your home. The key points to keep in mind is that the supplies should be easily accessed and kept organized so you can find what you need in a hurry.

## FIRST AID SUPPLIES

To a certain degree, what you keep on hand at home for medical needs will have to vary from family to family, based on individual needs, preferences, and other circumstances. But even so, there are some basics that are universal.

# ✚ CAUTION!

Whenever possible, seek competent medical assistance. Even if you're able to handle an injury at home during a crisis, see a doctor or visit an emergency room at the earliest opportunity to follow up and ensure there's nothing else that needs to be done. No book can ever take the place of trained medical professionals.

## WOUND CARE

There are a variety of injuries the home medic may need to face and they should be accounted for in the first aid kit. From cuts and scrapes to sprains and strains, plus burns and bruises, there's a lot that can happen and you should be ready for all of them.

- Adhesive bandages (variety of sizes)

- Gauze pads

- Athletic tape

- Super glue (good for expedient wound closure)

- Steri strips

- Butterfly bandages

- Antiseptic wash

- Antibiotic ointment

- Instant ice pack

- Ace bandages

- Burn cream or gel

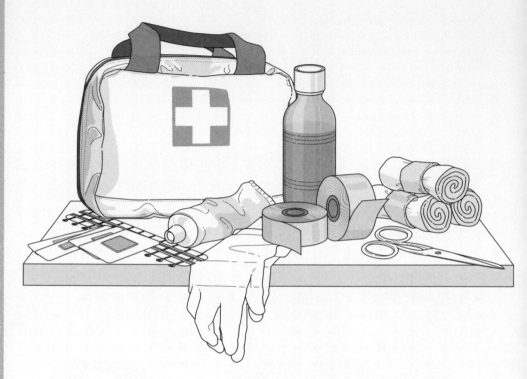

For severe injuries, you will want to add the following items:

- Tourniquet

- Hemostatic gauze

- Emergency, or Israeli Bandage

- Chest seal

- Zip stitch sutures

All of these are the sorts of supplies you should want to have in a clearly labeled and easily found container. If you're in need of a tourniquet, the last thing you want is to have people fumbling around the house, trying to find one.

## ⊕
# FEMININE
## HYGIENE PRODUCTS AREN'T FOR FIRST AID!

Time and again, you'll find this quasi-advice shared online – you can use tampons to treat gunshot wounds. Sure, at first blush, it kind of makes sense. Plug a bleeding hole with a product that's made to soak up blood in a body cavity. However, the idea breaks down quickly when you apply reasoning and science.

The wound channel from a gunshot injury won't be consistent in size and instead may get larger the farther in it goes. There's liable to be a whole lot going on inside the wound, way more than a tampon is designed to handle. Even a heavy-flow tampon will only hold about 2½ teaspoons (or about 12 ml) of fluid. That's barely a drop compared to how much blood you may be dealing with when it comes to a serious injury such as a gunshot wound.

## PERSONAL PROTECTIVE EQUIPMENT

One of the key points of rendering aid is to first protect yourself. This means donning the appropriate gear before diving in to the situation.

- Nitrile gloves

- CPR barrier

- Safety glasses

A word about gloves. If you can't afford to buy multiple sizes in quantity, opt for the largest size you'd need for someone in the house, typically large or extra-large. Someone with small hands can make do with a larger glove but it is just about impossible for someone with large hands to use small gloves.

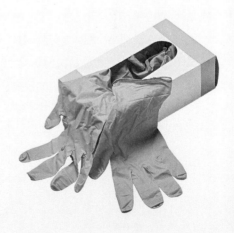

## MEDICATIONS

There are a few different types of medications you should keep on hand so that you're able to handle common ailments. I'd hazard to guess that most homes have at least some of these just as a matter of course, but perhaps this list will serve as a reminder of what needs to be replenished.

- Pain relievers / fever reducers

- Antidiarrheal

- Laxative

- Acid reducer

- Migraine relief

- Cold/flu symptom relief

If anyone in the home takes prescription medications, it is important to have an emergency supply available. In a crisis, you probably won't have the ability to run to the store for a refill. There are a couple of ways to augment your supply at home. Start by asking your physician if he or she can write you a prescription for an emergency supply. Many will do so, however not if the medication is a controlled substance like a narcotic. Also keep in mind that your insurance company may not cover the bill, so you could be on the hook for the additional meds.

Another way to handle it, although this method takes a little while, is to slowly build up the supply over time. With most prescriptions, you're able to refill it at least a few days before the current supply runs out. Use this overlap to your advantage. To make the math easy, we'll say that you have a medication you take once a day and you can refill it five days before it runs out. The day you get the refill, set five pills aside from the new supply and use the rest as prescribed. When you get your next refill, take ten pills from it for your emergency supply. Add the five older pills to your current bottle and use them as usual. Within a few months, you'll be able to build up enough of a stash to last at least a few weeks, if necessary. The key is to always use

the oldest pills first and save the newest ones.

Antibiotics are a common topic when it comes to preppers and medications. While antibiotics can be important when it comes to treating infection, it is just as crucial to know which antibiotics should be used with which types of infections. They are not universal. You also need to know the proper dosage and treatment cycle. If you're determined to stock up on antibiotics and you have a legal way to do so, I would highly encourage you to pick up a copy of *Alton's Antibiotics and Infectious Disease* by Joe Alton, M.D. It is an excellent resource for the layman. It explains which medications should be used and when and how.

## DENTAL EMERGENCIES

There are few things worse than a bad toothache, especially on a Friday night when the dental office opening on Monday seems like a lifetime away. I cannot stress enough the importance of dental health and wellness. Don't ignore issues; get them treated as soon as practical before they get much worse. If you're unable to afford what's needed, see if the provider will work with you on a payment plan. Failing that, see if there are any dental schools in your area.

Most of them offer discounted care provided by the students while under the supervision of a licensed dentist.

For times when you can't get to the dentist, here's what you should keep at home.

- Lidocaine

- Clove oil

- Temporary cavity filler

- Dental mirror

# ✚
# VET MEDS

In recent years, it has become something of a common practice for preppers and survivalists to seek out alternate methods of obtaining antibiotics, particularly the use of medicines that are marketed for use on animals. It has become so common, in fact, that some retailers won't stock them any longer, and some of the ones that do require a prescription.

Here's the thing. Most of these medications are indeed identical in makeup to the ones prescribed for humans. They're made in the same facilities with the same ingredients. However, far too many people use antibiotics improperly, leading to even worse problems.

If you decide to go down this route, use extreme caution.

## MEDICAL EQUIPMENT

You're not setting up a hospital room at home, but there are a few items that will be handy to have available in many situations. Again, you may already have some or all of these at home, but it pays to double-check and also to make sure they're all in the same place so they can be located easily.

- Thermometer

- Blood pressure cuff

- Pulse oximeter

- Tweezers

- Magnifying glass

- Small flashlight

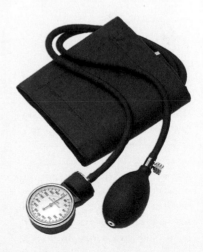

## HYGIENE

I don't know if cleanliness is truly next to godliness, but I can tell you that keeping at least reasonably clean works well to reduce the possibility of illness and infection. While disasters aren't known for being neat and tidy affairs, that doesn't mean you have to give up all pretense of being civilized.

## WASTE DISPOSAL

If the water isn't running, that doesn't necessarily mean you can't use your toilet. If you have the means to refill the tank, the toilet will flush. However, you should not sacrifice any of your supply of clean water. You could use melted snow, collected rainwater, or water pulled from a backyard pool for this purpose.

If that's not feasible, you can empty the bowl and then line it with a heavy-duty trash bag. You can sprinkle in some baking soda or powdered laundry detergent after each use to help cut down on offending odors. Use caution with this approach and change the bag often. The last thing you want is for an overloaded trash bag filled with human waste to burst open while you're carrying it through the house to take it outside – especially when you don't have running water to help with the cleanup.

# CONTRACEPTIVES

Let's face facts. There are all kinds of ways to spend time when the power is out and some of them could lead to fairly substantial changes to the family several months later. Keep a stash of the birth control supplies of your choice, just in case.

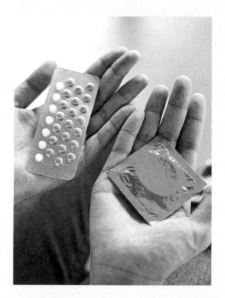

# HOMEMADE
## HAND SANITIZER

You can extend your water supply by creating your own homemade hand sanitizer to use in place of soap and water. It won't be as good as actually washing your hands but it'll do in a pinch. Keep the ingredients on hand for use when crisis strikes.

- Aloe vera gel

- Rubbing alcohol

- Essential oils

Start with about 4 tablespoons of aloe vera gel. You can find it in most health and beauty departments. Add 1 tablespoon of rubbing alcohol. Then, add 10 or so drops of your favorite essential oil. Tea tree oil is known for being a great germ fighter but the scent can be a bit strong for some folks. Peppermint might be nicer on the nose.

You can find small squeeze bottles for sale at the dollar store and elsewhere. Being a gel, your homemade concoction won't want to pour nicely into the container. You can use a small funnel and kind of shove the gel into the bottle using a straw or similar implement. Or, if you have one available, spoon the gel into a small plastic bag. Then, cut off the corner of the bag and squeeze the gel into the container. We've done this same thing using frosting to decorate cakes at home.

If need be, you can substitute witch hazel for the alcohol. Incidentally, aloe vera gel works wonders on burns, including sunburn, so it is great to have on hand whether you're making hand sanitizer or not.

Of course, camping stores sell all manner of chemical toilets, along with the supplies needed for them. They work well, if you have the space to store them when they're not needed.

Urban residents typically don't have the luxury of acres and acres of land where they can bury waste. Instead, the waste can be bagged up and placed in the trash for later pick up.

While we're on the subject, we all remember the Great Toilet Paper Shortage of 2020, right? If you have the space for it, I recommend keeping enough of it on hand at all times to last a full two weeks to a month. While there are alternatives, most of them are less than ideal. That said, many families have invested in bidet attachments for their toilets and have grown to appreciate them immensely. However, those won't work if the water isn't flowing, so keep that in the back of your mind.

## BATHING

Imagine being stuck at home for several weeks after a disaster hits and there's no running water. It is the height of summer and air-conditioning is just a fond memory at this point. You and your family are constantly sweaty, dirty, and just plain gross. Toss an infant into the mix, one that's going through a dozen diapers a day. The level of stink being generated in that home could probably be weaponized.

It is best to plan ahead to have some means of cleaning up. Baby wipes are a good start. They're good for quick sponge baths and won't take up much space for storage. Never flush them, however, even if they're labeled as being safe for doing so. Just toss them in the trash.

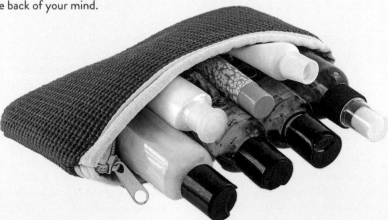

Try to always keep extra soap and shampoo stockpiled, at least enough to last a few weeks. The same goes for toothpaste, dental floss, and mouthwash.

Avoid using body sprays and scented deodorants in grid down scenarios. Trust me, after raising three teenage boys, body sprays are highly overrated when it comes to masking other smells.

A camp shower wouldn't be the worst investment. You can find one at camping and sporting goods stores. It consists of a black plastic bag that holds a few gallons of water. It is filled and hung up outside so the sun can heat the water inside. A short hose with a spigot is attached to the bottom of the bag. You use that to get wet and rinse off.

## LAUNDRY

This probably won't be a big problem in a short-term situation, but if it extends beyond several days, you might start running low on clean socks and undergarments. One of the best DIY solutions is to make a hand-powered washing machine from a plastic bucket and a toilet plunger.

STEP 1: Start with a clean 5-gallon bucket with a lid. You'll also need a new, and thus clean, rubber toilet plunger. Cut a hole in the middle of the bucket lid large enough for the plunger handle to fit through easily.

STEP 2: Next, use a razor knife to cut three or four holes in the rubber end of the plunger. The holes should be about the size of a quarter.

STEP 3: To use, toss a few pair of socks or underwear, maybe a shirt as well, into the bucket and fill it with enough water to cover them by 4 or 5 inches. Add in a little laundry detergent, then put in the plunger. Slide the lid over the plunger handle and secure it.

STEP 4: Work the plunger up and down. This is the agitator in your new washing machine. Move it side to side too. Once you feel the clothes are about as clean as you can probably get them, take them out and empty the bucket.

STEP 5: Refill with water and rinse the clothes, then wring them out and lay them somewhere to dry.

Incidentally, this is a great chore for the kids in the house who keep complaining that they're bored.

Being able to clean up, even on a limited basis, isn't just healthy; it is good for morale. Anything you can do to keep the mood in the home elevated is a good thing during a disaster.

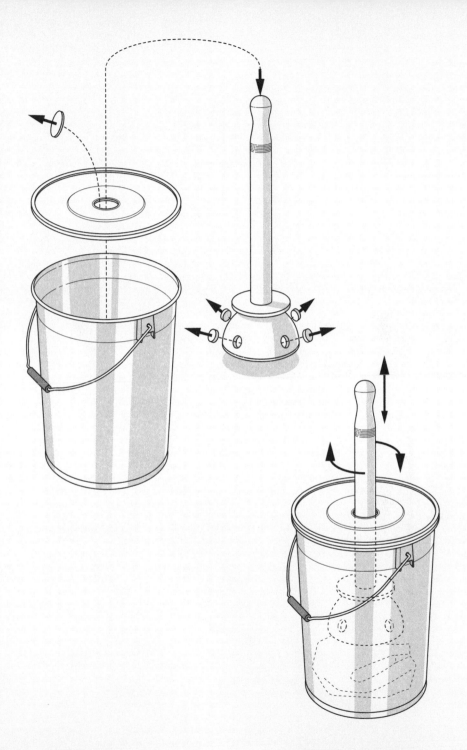

# CHAPTER 5
# SECURITY

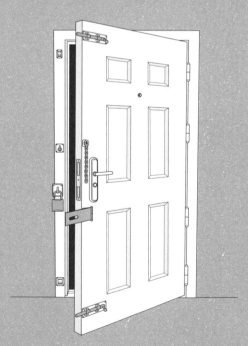

**ALL OF THE STOCKPILED SUPPLIES IN THE WORLD WON'T DO YOU MUCH GOOD IF SOMEONE CAN TAKE THEM AWAY FROM YOU. IF THINGS TAKE A TURN AND GET UGLY, ONLY THOSE WHO CAN PROTECT THEIR HOMES AND SUPPLIES WILL BE ABLE TO KEEP THEM. EVEN WHEN TIMES ARE MORE OR LESS NORMAL, THERE'S RISK OF HOME INVASION, ROBBERY, ASSAULT, AND OTHER UNPLEASANTNESS.**

## OPSEC

This is an acronym that has been shortened from Operations Security. The term originated with the military and had a specific meaning relating to the protection of vital information. It has, however, subsequently been co-opted by the prepper community and come to be something of a blanket term related to keeping your supplies and your plans as private as possible.

In short, as the saying goes, loose lips sink ships. Keep your preps to yourself and encourage family members to also keep things quiet.

The concern is that if others in your area know you have extra, they might come looking for it. Personally, I have no problem with helping others. I just want to be able to make the decision for myself on who gets helped and how much is

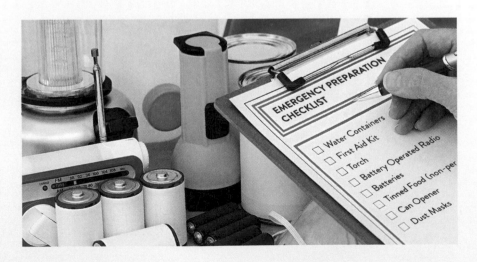

provided to them, instead of just about anyone knocking on my door looking to take what they want by force.

Here are a few ways to avoid being too overt or obvious about your prepping.

- Keep food and other supplies stored out of sight.

- If you have a garage, park inside it and close the door before unloading your car after shopping.

- Store your vehicle emergency kit in the trunk, or hidden in some other way.

Talking about preparedness to family and friends can feel like a double-edged sword. You want to encourage them to be prepared for emergencies, but at the same time you don't necessarily want them showing up at your doorstep looking for a handout, simply because they know you probably have extra food stored away somewhere. Some will even go so far as to say, "I'll just head over to your place if something happens!"

The best approach to counteracting that might be honesty. Explain to them that you have limited space and even more limited resources. It would be better for everyone involved if they would work on getting their own preps in order, instead of simply planning to rely

on you. Tell them you're glad to help them through the process, but there's just no practical way there would be enough room for them to hunker down at your place.

## SECURITY PLANS

Whether we're talking about a studio apartment, a skyscraper, or a rural homestead, every security plan has these three elements in common:

- Deter

- Delay

- Defend

They work like phases, with one leading to the next.

## DETER

A burglar, just like most human beings, makes decisions based on risk versus reward. Will he find enough inside the home worth stealing to offset the possibility of getting caught? They're often lazy and they want easy targets. If you can convince them that your home isn't worth the effort it'll take to get inside, you've won the battle before it started.

The idea here is twofold; you should downplay the anticipated reward while increase the perceived risk.

For example, if you purchase a new TV, don't just haul the empty

cardboard box to the curb for collection. Cut it up and slip the pieces into bags so that they aren't visible. Don't leave valuables such as jewelry, purses, wallets, in easy view of the front door or any ground level windows. Keep your vehicles locked when you're not in them.

For the risk side of the equation, what you want to do is make your home appear as though it will take a fair amount of work just to get inside undetected. Install motion-activated lights near the front and rear doors, so nobody can sneak in after dark. They also work as an alert system for you. If you notice the light in the backyard turns on, get up and see what triggered it.

Sure, most of the time it'll probably be a raccoon or other nocturnal four-legged critter. But, if it is one of the two-legged variety, you'll want to know about it.

Remove large shrubs and bushes that could hide someone while they try to break in through windows.

If you're determined to keep greenery near the house, consider something that will be less than pleasant to be around, such as hawthorn, which has thorns.

Signs indicating the use of alarm or security systems can be great deterrents. The presence of a loud dog works great, too.

# SIGNS
## AND STICKERS

Many people like to advertise the fact that they own firearms with signs or stickers bearing clever sayings, such as:

• This house is protected by Smith & Wesson!

• Burglars will be shot, survivors will be shot again.

• Warning – Nothing here is worth your life.

These and similar slogans, while amusing, do exactly nothing to deter thieves. In fact, these signs can do the opposite, because they inform all who see them that there are probably firearms, which are expensive and easily sold, located inside the home. All the enterprising burglar has to do is wait for everyone to be gone. While you might have all of the firearms locked down tight, the crook might find other goodies to snatch while they're in the house.

# FOILING
## PORCH PIRATES

In recent years, the prevalence of people stealing packages from porches and front doors has skyrocketed. If you're not home when the package is delivered, there's a chance you'll never get a chance to open it. There are a few options to mitigate this risk.

1 If it is practical, consider having all packages delivered to you at work. It isn't an ideal solution for everyone, but for some it works well.

2 If you receive a high number of packages regularly, renting a post office box might be worth the investment. You don't need to rent a large box, either; just get the smallest one available, because that's the cheapest. Anything that won't fit will be held at the desk for you, with a notice slipped into the box. Some locations have large lockers where packages are placed, with the key put into your box for retrieval.

3 You could partner with neighbors. Let them know you have a package being delivered and, if they would be kind enough to grab it for you, that would be great.

Installing a camera that has a view of the front porch is great for capturing an image of the thief, but it won't truly protect your packages from being swiped.

## DELAY

If, despite your best efforts to convince them that the risk outweighs the rewards, the ne'er-do-well decides your home is their next target, the longer it takes for them to get inside, the better. The more time they have to spend working their way toward their goal, the more time you have to become aware of their presence and take whatever action you feel is necessary.

This is where hardening the home comes into play. We want to make things as difficult as possible for the thief. If you live in a rental, you'll probably want to have a talk with your landlord about some of your plans here, but most of what we will be discussing is not only discreet but won't cause any damage to the property.

Start with entry doors. Make sure the locks work and use them every time you leave the house. Some people go as far as keeping doors locked at all times, even when they're home. This isn't the worst idea. Install deadbolts if you don't have them. The bolt should extend at least one full inch (2.5 cm) into the doorframe.

Most doors are hung using relatively short screws to attach the hinges to the frame. This means these are weak connections and the door could be kicked in.

Remove just one of those screws and take it to the hardware store. Pick up steel wood screws that are about three inches long (7.5 cm) and the same diameter as the hinge screw you brought. Replace the hinge screws one at a time with the longer ones. These will provide a much stronger, more secure connection. By swapping them one at a time, you will avoid the need to rehang the door.

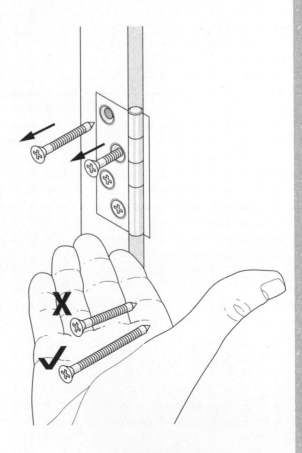

Keep windows locked when they aren't opened to allow airflow. Consider installing security film on at least the ground level windows. The film won't make the glass totally unbreakable, but it will prevent the glass from shattering and should withstand several hard strikes with a hammer or other object. Again, the goal here is to slow them down before they get inside. Film such as this is a great way to strengthen windows without obstructing the view.

The use of a camera system and motion sensors can also go a long way toward alerting you to the presence of possible trouble. However, keep in mind that alarms, cameras, and other such devices might not work at all if the power goes out.

If you have a garage, keep it secure. Any vehicle that parks outside the garage for the night should not have a garage door opener in it. Take it into the house with you when you park the car. Otherwise, if someone were to break into the vehicle, having access to that remote means they could easily enter your home as well.

Many people end up using their garage for storage instead of for a vehicle. If you don't need to be able to open the garage door from the outside on a regular basis, secure it. A simple plastic zip tie will do the

# TIPS FOR
## SECURE BUILDINGS

If you live in an apartment complex or similar kind of building, there should be plenty of lighting around entrances as well as in parking areas. If there isn't, talk to the building management about it.

Don't let anyone piggyback on your entrance, meaning if the exterior door to the building is locked, don't let someone else come in with you unless you know them to be a fellow resident. This is one of the primary ways crooks and thieves will gain access to a secure building.

Part of the move-in process should involve the landlord installing new locks on your door. If they don't offer it up the lease, ask to have it added. The previous resident may still have a copy of their old key it could be used to gain access to your unit.

If one doesn't exist, consider starting a Facebook page or other social media site for your building and inviting residents to join it. This is a great way to get to know one another as well as share tips and information.

# HIDING
## IN PLAIN SIGHT

One more delay tactic is to make it difficult for the burglar or home invader to find the valuables they are seeking. The master bedroom is often their first stop, because it is instinctual for us to want to keep precious belongings close to us. Hence, this is where people tend to keep cash, jewelry, firearms, and other important items. Instead, make judicious use of other areas of your home.

**BASEMENT:** If you go downstairs and look up, unless you have a dropped ceiling installed, you'll be looking at wiring as well as PVC pipe here and there. Most casual observers would never notice an extra run of the latter. You can fit a considerable amount into even a short length of 4-inch (10-cm) PVC. Install a threaded cap on the ends so you can easily open it and remove what you have inside.

**ATTIC:** If you mark a few boxes with, "Grandma's clothes" or something similar, most burglars won't give them a second glance. Just make sure family members know to check inside the boxes before donating them to a thrift store.

**LIVING ROOM:** Emergency cash can be hidden inside photo frames. Just tape the paper money to the back of the photos. Make sure you use cheap plastic frames so burglars don't nab them thinking they're silver or something worth money.

**KITCHEN:** Cash can be placed in envelopes and taped to the underside of utensil drawers. Don't, however, put it in the freezer. Experienced crooks will know to look there.

**BATHROOM:** There is a number of diversion safes on the market that are geared toward the bathroom. These are small storage containers that are made to look like a can of shaving cream, deodorant, or something similar. Thieves are well aware of these products, so probably best to pass on them.

trick. Just loop it through the track and a part of the metal frame of the door and pull it tight. Another option is to fit a screwdriver through the track to stop the wheels on the door from rolling through it. Both of these are easy to remove when you do want to open the door from the inside.

If you have windows in the garage, consider installing shades or applying window darkening film to the glass so people cannot see inside.

## DEFEND

When push comes to shove, you might have to take action against an intruder. It is a good idea to be familiar with the laws in your area regarding what you are and are not allowed to do in defense of your home. While yes, the safety of your family is paramount and from that perspective anything goes, you can avoid hassles with law enforcement and attorneys down the road if you know ahead of time what the law says regarding self-defense and related issues.

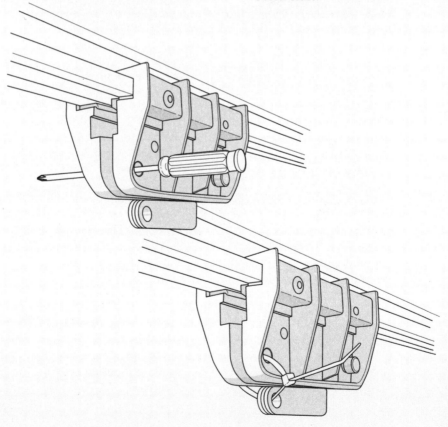

The best thing you can do in this regard is to invest time, energy, and expense into training. If you're going to pick up a weapon, know how to use it properly and effectively. Plinking at the range is one thing. Hitting the target in chaotic, low light conditions when your heart is pounding and you feel like you're about to fill your shorts is another thing entirely.

Speaking of low light, that will probably be one of your biggest issues in a defense situation at home, if a break in happens at night. You can mitigate it by installing motion-sensitive nightlights in the hallways. They'll give off just enough light to see what you're doing without blinding you. Plus, small children will appreciate them for middle of the night trips to the bathroom.

Make sure you know the applicable laws in your area regarding defense of self, family, and home. More than one homeowner has ended up on the wrong side of a lawsuit because they went too far with the use of force. While you might considering shooting and hitting a burglar a win, if you didn't follow the laws in effect at the time of the incident, you could lose everything defending yourself in court.

## WEAPONS

There are several options available when it comes to arming yourself. Consider your physical abilities as well as your location and the laws that are in force regarding weapons. You absolutely do not want to run afoul of law enforcement simply because you wanted to be able to protect yourself.

### FIREARMS

As a general rule, a firearm is the ideal defense weapon. It lets you to keep distance between you and the attacker and, for the most part, the use of a firearm isn't limited by physical strength. As the old saying goes, "God made man, but Sam Colt made them equal." The current accepted recommendation favors an AR-style rifle for home defense. It is relatively easy to wield and control, has little recoil, and basic proficiency isn't difficult to obtain with some practice.

A handgun, of course, is smaller and easier to carry than a rifle on a regular basis. With some range time, accuracy at short distances is fairly easy to manage.

Once upon a time, the shotgun was the preferred home defense weapon. For some, it still is. However, compared to other options, you're limited in the number of shots you have available before reloading. The weapon is also larger than an AR rifle, with substantially greater recoil, at least at the 12-gauge level.

The importance of regular practice and training with a firearm cannot be overemphasized. Just plinking at tin cans at the range isn't enough. If possible, seek out tactical-style training that involves movement as well as simulated chaotic conditions.

## KNIVES

A sharp blade, and this category would also include any number of similar implements that are designed to puncture or pierce, is a common choice for a primary or backup defense weapon. Here's the trouble: By their very nature, they require you to be up close and personal to your attacker. If you're close enough to use a knife against that person, he or she is close enough to grab you, which is not an enviable position.

Plus, it takes a certain mindset to use a knife against another person. It isn't easy to cut and stab someone and hesitation could cost

you dearly. However, most people will think twice about risking a knife injury.

It isn't like you see in the movies. There are few moves with a knife that involve the person just falling to the ground instantly. Instead, you're waiting for them to bleed out, which will take some time. One approach I recommend is to do what you can to attack their bodily structure. If you're able to cut a tendon or major muscle, that limb won't function as well. I highly recommend seeking out proper training. One excellent resource is Martial Blade Concepts (MartialBladeConcepts.com).

# TRAPS

So, you're thinking of setting up some kind of surprise for anyone who tries to break in? You might want to think again. Booby traps – the kind that can injure, maim, or kill – are generally a very bad idea, for a couple of reasons.

Traps are indiscriminate; they cannot tell the difference between you, a burglar, your child, or a firefighter coming in to save you if your home is ablaze. If the trap is triggered, it will go off no matter who or what is responsible.

In most areas such traps are illegal and can lead to hefty lawsuits. The classic example is the Katko vs. Briney court case decided by Iowa Supreme Court back in 1971. Bertha Briney inherited an old farmhouse and it stood vacant for several years. It was boarded up and they'd put up several "No Trespassing" signs. Marvin Katko was a local gas station attendant who was familiar with the farmhouse he often hunted in the area. He and a buddy of his had even been in the house, stealing antique fruit jars and other items.

Frustrated with the thefts, Edward Briney mounted a shotgun in the house that would fire when a door was opened. He aimed it downward so as to shoot an intruder's legs instead of their chest or head.

On July 16, 1967, Katko broke in and triggered the trap. He lost much of his right leg due to the shotgun blast and only survived because a friend got him to a hospital, where he stayed for more than a month recovering from his wounds.

The court ruled that deadly force was not justified in the protection of property. Had either of the Brineys been in the home at the time, the situation may have been different. Katko sued the Brineys and won $20,000 in actual damages and $10,000 in punitive damages. That $30,000 total was awarded back in 1971. Adjusted to 2021, that's about $202,000. That also doesn't take into account the legal fees incurred by the Brineys.

I can think of a number of better ways to spend $200K.

## PEPPER SPRAY

This is what we typically consider a less-than-lethal defense option. Used properly, it will temporarily incapacitate the bad guy or gal, giving you time to get away. The active ingredient in pepper spray is capsaicin, which is derived from plants such as chili peppers. When sprayed into someone's face, it causes the mucous membranes in the eyes, nose, and throat to become inflamed. As a practical matter, it makes it difficult for the person to see or breathe.

Opt for a delivery system that streams the chemical, instead of a fog or spray. The latter will probably come back to bite you, especially in breezy conditions. Plus, the stream is easier to aim.

## ELECTROSHOCK

There are two primary options in this category. Stun guns have two probes extending from the weapon. When you touch them both to someone's skin and activate the weapon, it sends a shock into the person. They can work well, but, as with knives, you'll need to be within arm's length of the person because you must make physical contact with him or her.

The Taser fires two hooked metal probes at the attacker. They're connected to the weapon by wires. Once the probes are embedded in the person, a shock is sent via the wires. The downside is that thick clothing can be problematic because the probes may not penetrate to the skin.

FUN FACT: Taser is an acronym. It stands for Tom A Swift Electric Rifle, named after the protagonist of a series of novels written for children that was first published in the early 1900s.

# WASP SPRAY
## IS NOT
## RECOMMENDED

For the last several years, the idea of using wasp spray instead of pepper spray has been floating around the Internet. I'm not certain where it began, but it is one of those urban legends that just won't die.

As anyone who has received some blowback when spraying bugs will tell you, it might sting a little but that's about it. It is absolutely no substitute for pepper spray. Not only does it not work well against people, it is also illegal to use for this purpose, because it is a violation of the Federal Insecticide, Fungicide, and Rodenticide Act.

Now, that said, if you're attacked in the garage and the closest thing within reach is a can of wasp spray, aim for their face and let loose, then take off to a safer location. However, that's not the same as stashing a can of spray in every room of the house so you always have it within reach in case someone breaks in.

## SITUATIONAL AWARENESS

This is perhaps the greatest asset you can have when it comes to personal security. In short, it boils down to being aware of your surroundings. Instead of keeping your face buried in your phone as you move about your day, keep your head on a swivel and pay attention to the world around you.

It will help you to be in a better position to recognize potential threats and take action as necessary. It might be as simple as crossing to the other side of the street to avoid problems with a group of people arguing with one another up ahead.

Another advantage of keeping your head up and looking around is that it projects an air of self-confidence. Muggers and other undesirables prey on the weak. If you look assured and confident, they will probably leave you alone and seek a different victim.

# CHAPTER 6
# COMMUNICATION

**WHEN IT COMES TO HANDLING A DISASTER OR CRISIS EFFECTIVELY, YOU NEED TO BE ABLE TO MAKE INFORMED DECISIONS ABOUT THE SITUATION. BY DEFINITION, DOING SO REQUIRES INFORMATION, WHICH IS WHAT COMMUNICATION IS ALL ABOUT. WHEN YOU GET RIGHT DOWN TO IT, COMMUNICATION IS SIMPLY TRANSMITTING AND RECEIVING INFORMATION, IDEALLY IN AN EASILY UNDERSTOOD FORMAT.**

The information you're able to gather may be the deciding factor on whether you should hunker down and wait it out or hit the road and hightail it for your bugout location. It might allow you to get out ahead of the crowd. Either way, it could give you the advantage of knowing what's on the way in terms of hazards and give you time to prepare for them.

The trick, of course, is planning ahead so that you're able to communicate, both near and far, and keep apprised of what's going on around you. Fortunately, there are several options. The ideal solution is to have some variety in your chosen methods instead of relying on a single one. Take into account your budget, familiarity with technology, and ease of use when shopping.

## TWO-WAY COMMUNICATION

One of the key elements of two-way communication is the ability to ask questions and clarify information. When you watch TV or listen to a news report on the radio, you're limited to what they tell you. They may inadvertently omit a piece of information that for you is particularly important or even critical.

Being able to request more information, ideally from a source you know to be trustworthy, is a luxury that you cannot overlook.

### CELL PHONE

For most folks, the first thing grabbed for communication is a cell phone, even if they don't use them much for calling anymore. Text messaging as well as any number of social media apps allow for instant communication anywhere a signal can be had. Which, of course, is the crux of the matter. One of the first thing affected in a catastrophe is that signal. Depending on the nature of the disaster, it could be that the cell towers become compromised. Even if they're still working, they might be overwhelmed by the sheer number of people trying to get in touch with others.

# ZELLO

In the last several years, Zello has risen to become one of the most popular communication apps available. In the wake of Hurricane Katrina hitting the southern United States in 2005, Zello was used by several rescue agencies, as well as amateur volunteers. As a result, it was featured in many news stories and became widely recommended.

Zello operates much like a walkie talkie, where you "push to talk" and then wait for a response. It also has the ability to replay messages you've received, so you can listen again for an address or other needed details.

However, there's something many people don't understand about Zello and similar apps. They still need a way to access the Internet in order to function. Without Wi-Fi or data service from your cell provider, Zello isn't going to work.

If the signal is weak or if the network seems to be overloaded, try texting instead of attempting to make voice calls. A text message will often make it through where a call cannot. If you're able to get online and utilize a social media service to send or receive messages, so much the better.

One thing I recommend every person carry in their pocket, purse, EDC bag, or wherever, is a charging cord for their phone as well as a USB to AC adapter. Both of these items are inexpensive, but could prove priceless in an urban area during a crisis. All too often, we find that just when we truly need our phone, that's when it is down to about 12 percent battery. If you have the space, a small battery pack is also a great idea. But if not, having the cord and wall adapter gives you options when you're out and about.

## SOCIAL MEDIA
For good or ill, we have become incredibly reliant on social media such as Facebook and Twitter, to keep in touch with people as well as gather news and stay up to date on current events. Provided you have an Internet signal, this will probably continue during and after a disaster strikes.

You can use it not only to request and gather information but also to update your own status so family and friends know if you're okay or in need of assistance.

## AMATEUR RADIO

Known as ham radio, this network of radios and operators often serves as the backbone for emergency communication during a disaster. There is a learning curve with the equipment as well as studying involved to obtain the necessary license to use it.

There are some who say they're not going to worry about the license, because the applicable agencies probably won't be enforcing those regulations during a disaster. While this may be true, the license is needed to practice with the equipment beforehand, which is a necessary step in the learning process. Not to mention the networking you're able to do with other ham operators ahead of a real emergency.

Make no mistake, you can listen all you want. The license is only required if you will be transmitting over the air. However, the latter is how you'll connect with other operators now, as well as how you'll be able to share information in the wake of an event.

You can get by without a huge investment in gear, although the sky is the limit if it becomes a serious interest. Many ham operators end up with entire rooms devoted to equipment and spend hours every week talking to people all over the globe.

What I recommend as a starting place is to seek out a local ham radio club in your local area. In the United States alone, there are more than 700,000 licensed ham operators, and odds are good that there's a club in your area. Almost all operators are extremely helpful to those new to the hobby.

Knowing the role ham radio can play in disaster communications, many clubs as well as individual operators will regularly practice using their equipment in less than optimum conditions, such as improvising antennas and such.

## CITIZEN'S BAND (CB) RADIO

These days, CB radio is largely used by professional drivers, such as delivery trucks, semi-trucks, and the like. For a brief period in the 1970s, though, it was all the rage, largely influenced by movies such as *Convoy* and *Smokey and the Bandit*. Almost overnight, every car and truck driver in North America had a clever or funny CB handle or nickname, and the airwaves were filled with slang such as "bear in the air" and "go-go juice."

By the early to mid-1980s, the popularity has died off considerably. Today, with the advent of cell phones and other communication tools, CB is back to being mostly used by road truck drivers. One major downside to these radios is the limited range. At most, we're talking roughly 20 miles, and it can be considerably less, depending upon terrain.

The other drawback is that the communication isn't private. If someone is having a conversation on channel 8, anyone with a radio in range tuned to that channel can hear everything being said. Given that there only 40 channels from which to choose, it doesn't take much for someone to scan through them all and see who might be talking. Plus, with the range limitation, they'll know that whomever they hear is in the immediate area.

Where it shines, however, is that truck drivers may have information others do not, simply because they're on the road and have a unique vantage point as a result. The equipment is relatively inexpensive, too. So, while I wouldn't suggest it as any kind of primary means of communication, if the budget allows, it wouldn't be a bad addition to your preps, simply as relatively local data-gathering tool.

# RADIO
## SCANNERS

For many years, an exciting hobby has been to listen to a scanner that picks up local law enforcement and emergency services radio traffic. You learn quickly that people call the police for a mind-boggling array of reasons that go well beyond potential law breaking, including helping a parent to convince their child to take their cold medicine and handling a dispute between two elderly gentlemen who are arguing about who won a specific baseball World Series.

Many agencies have gone to digital transmissions in the last several years. You can still listen to them, but you have to use a special type of scanner to do so. Or, you can use an app and get the broadcasts over your cell phone or computer.

These transmissions can be incredibly useful in a disaster or crisis. They could give you a heads up on situations such as road closures or ongoing instances of civil unrest.

When investing in any radio equipment, make sure to pick up at least a couple of sets of spare batteries for the gear.

## HANDHELD RADIOS

These have come a long way since we were kids playing army in the woods, using cheap plastic radios to fill each other in on "enemy" movements. The two-way radios in use today operate using either Family Radio Service (FRS) or General Mobile Radio Service (GMRS) frequencies.

To avoid getting too deep into the weeds with the technical side of things, here's what you need to know about the differences between the two types of radios. As a general rule of thumb, GMRS radios have greater range than FRS radios. However, GMRS requires a license from the FCC (Federal Communications Commission), whereas FRS does not.

Whichever type you pursue, ignore whatever the package says in terms of advertised range. The only way several miles is realistic is if you're in a desert and there's absolutely nothing between you and the other radio. In an urban area, rife with tall buildings and

other structures, you'll be lucky if you manage to get a range of several city blocks in most cases.

That being the case, the only real use these would have for the urban prepper is to stay in touch with neighbors.

Take the scenario of two people exactly the same, except there is a building in between. It blocks the dotted line and there is a cross showing the radios aren't working.

## MEDIA SOURCES

As we said at the outset, the major drawback of one-way communication tools is that you're limited to the information they decide to share with you. There's no way to dig deeper, at least not without using other means.

However, the advantage is that the media typically has access to a greater range of information sources than the average person. Also, government agencies will use

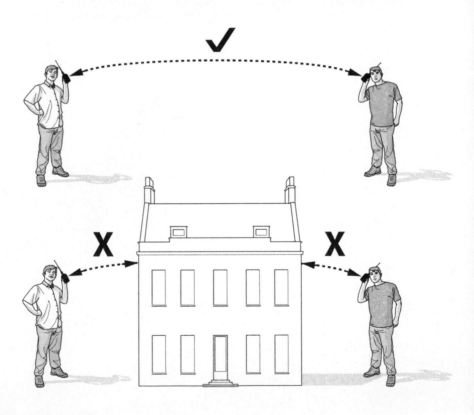

# NOAA
## WEATHER RADIO
## ALL HAZARDS

When we talk about weather radio, we usually think about situations such as tornado warnings. However, there's a lot more involved. Working with the FCC's Emergency Alert System (EAS), this radio network will broadcast any number of hazardous conditions that go well beyond severe weather, such as:

• Earthquakes

• Chemical spills

• 911 outages

• AMBER alerts

the media to make announcements. Even if they aren't telling the public everything, under the guise of safety, whatever they do share can be useful.

Invest in a good-quality emergency radio, one that will tune in weather radio broadcasts as well as AM and FM. It should be powered by batteries with a dynamo or crank backup. Many models will also be able to charge cell phones and other devices by USB.

## COMMUNICATIONS PLAN

I know it sounds obvious, but in the event of a crisis you will want to coordinate with your loved ones. The problem is that doing so might be easier said than done. Hopefully, it will be a simple matter of calling or texting. But as the saying goes, hope for the best and plan for the worst.

### THE 3-3-3 PLAN

This one is easy for people to remember. Every three hours (3:00, 6:00, 9:00, 12:00), at the top of the hour, tune the radio to Channel 3 and attempt contact for at least three minutes. The idea is that you're conserving power with the radio equipment, instead of it running it nonstop for hours on end.

What you deem to be Channel 3 is up to you. If you're using CB or handheld radios, that's easy. But otherwise, you can alter this to suit what you're using. The critical piece here is the targeted time frame for attempted communication. It doesn't need to be an actual Channel 3, just make sure everyone is on the same page as to what will be used.

# IN CASE
## OF EMERGENCY

**It is a wise idea to store at least one emergency contact in every cell phone and other device. Label it as ICE, which stands for In Case of Emergency. If something does happen and you're incapacitated, this is who rescue workers will try to reach.**

# CONTACT

Local phone lines can quickly become overloaded in a crisis, but you might have better luck reaching someone who isn't in your immediate area. As part of your overall communications plan, make arrangements with a trusted family member who lives out of town, ideally a fair distance away, to act as a communications hub. If you're not able to reach your immediate family members, call your out-of-town contact. Their job is to pass information back and forth and help everyone get connected again.

## RALLY POINT

Part of the communications plan needs to be instruction on what to do if you can't get in touch with each other. If home is not safe or reachable, there should be at least one offsite location designated as a rally point or meeting place for your family. The goal is to have everyone know where to go if home isn't a viable option.

Where you choose this location to be is up to you, but it should be a place familiar to everyone involved. It could be the home of a family member, or maybe a favorite restaurant. Choose a place that will probably be open and accessible.

# CHAPTER 7
# EVERY DAY CARRY (EDC)

**AN OFTEN-REPEATED MANTRA IN THE PREPPER WORLD IS THAT SKILLS TRUMP STUFF. MEANING, KNOWING HOW TO GET THE JOB DONE USING A VARIETY OF MEANS IS BETTER THAN JUST BUYING MORE AND MORE GEAR. THIS IS ABSOLUTELY TRUE AND, IF YOU HAVE TO CHOOSE BETWEEN EITHER LEARNING A NEW SKILL OR BUYING A SHINY NEW PIECE OF EQUIPMENT, GO WITH THE EDUCATION EVERY TIME.**

However, humankind invented tools for a reason. They make work easier. Sure, you could put together a bow drill and grind out an ember every time you need a new fire lit. Or, you could use a disposable lighter, a ferrocerium rod, or any number of other more modern approaches to achieve the same goal in less time and with less effort.

Understand, I'm not suggesting that there's little or no value in learning what we sometimes call "primitive" survival skills. Far from it, actually, because there's a lot to gain from mastering them, including a tremendous sense of self-confidence. But when we're talking about true survival, I believe that you should conserve your energy and resources as much as possible. Handicapping yourself at the outset by disallowing the use of modern gear isn't wise.

## EVERY DAY CARRY (EDC)

EDC is meant to refer to the items you keep with you on a daily basis, most often carried directly on your person. For many, the acronym means "everyday carry." I prefer to explain it as "every day carry" to emphasize that these are things you carry virtually every single day. Semantics, absolutely, but words matter.

The basic idea is to have a small assemblage of gear that you'll probably need throughout the day, saving you from having to find a certain tool when you're in the middle of a task.

Think of EDC as having layers. The first is what you carry on your person, such as in your pockets or on your belt. These are items you would have with you pretty much every time you leave the house, no matter where you're headed.

The next layer is what some call "off-body EDC." Many people carry some type of bag or pack with them on a daily basis. It could be a backpack or maybe a briefcase of some kind, used to shuffle a laptop and work papers back and forth. Even if you don't need such a conveyance for work purposes, you might choose to carry one anyway. If you're already carrying a bag, it only makes sense to devote a little space inside of it to survival or preparedness gear. We're not talking about a fully loaded expedition-size pack. Just a small shoulder bag or something similar would suffice for most folks.

The point to having the off-body EDC is to have the ability to carry more than you can comfortably fit in your pockets, and have it packed in a container that you keep close at hand throughout your day.

Of course, what you personally need or use on a daily basis will differ from one person to the next, at least slightly. That said, I wanted to cover the basic categories of common EDC gear, and give you an idea of what to look for when shopping for something to fill that slot.

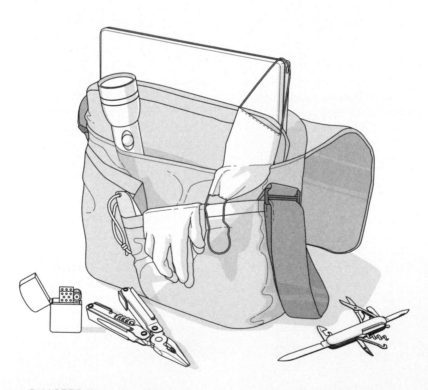

## KNIFE

A sharp edge is one of humankind's oldest tools. Over the centuries, it evolved from a piece of chipped obsidian to a finely crafted tool made from steel. Today, the choice starts with deciding if you want to carry a fixed blade knife or a folding knife. The advantage a fixed blade has over the folder is strength. Being one piece of steel, it lacks a joint or other potential failure point. But, depending on your job, your employer might frown upon you coming to work with a knife visible on your belt. However, there are fixed blade knives small enough to fit into a pocket, so there's that to consider too.

For the most part, urban residents can probably get by with a good-quality folding knife, such as something from Victorinox or Case Knives. These are nonthreatening to coworkers and will handle most routine chores just fine. We're not considering something for self-defense . We just want something that can open boxes, cut cordage, and handle similar tasks.

## FLASHLIGHT

I'll admit, I went years without carrying a pocket flashlight. I just didn't see the point, not until a friend of mine convinced me to try doing so for a few days. I picked up one from Streamlight and, by the end of the first day, I was a believer. Once you start carrying one, you'll be surprised how often you use it. From finding the dog toy under the couch to attaching booster cables to the car battery, having a small flashlight with you makes life easier.

The illumination capability is typically measured in lumens, with the higher the number, the more powerful the light. Something to keep in mind is that it is easy to think you need a much brighter light than is truly necessary. You just want to be able to navigate your way down a darkened hallway during a power outage, not cast shadow puppets on the lunar surface.

As a general rule of thumb, something around 50 lumens will probably be sufficient for most situations, although 100-200 lumens or so is better if you're checking the backyard for weird noises late at night. If you can source a flashlight that has variable output, so much the better.

# HOW MANY
## KNIVES DO
## YOU NEED?

Personally, I feel that if you will be carrying a knife as a defensive weapon, it shouldn't be the same one that you'll use to open packages and perform other routine tasks. So, with this in mind, if you go down that route it means carrying two knives at a minimum. For most people, that's plenty. However, those who favor high-end knives often carry a third as well. The extra one will be cheap and not in the greatest shape, with the sole purpose of being a knife they can lend out to people at work without worry.

## MULTITOOL

This one might be debatable for some people, because it is all too easy to end up with something that feels like a boat anchor on your belt. On the other hand, when you need a screwdriver, a pair of pliers, wire cutters, or another tool in a hurry, unless you're lugging a toolbox around, a multitool can probably get the job done.

In addition to weight, the other major downside is that while a multitool can do a lot of things, it can't do all of those things exceptionally well. Ever try to loosen a tight bolt using needle-nose pliers?

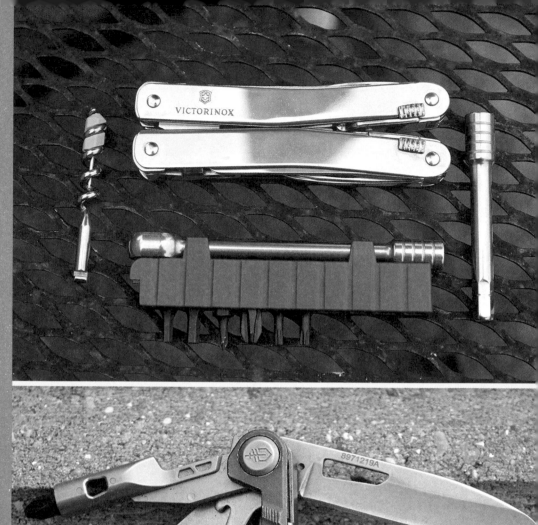

If you decide to invest in one, look for a model that won't weigh you down too much while still offering you the options you'll need most often. When I'm out and about in the city, I keep one in my EDC bag instead of on my belt or in a pocket.

## LIGHTER

Even if you're not a smoker, it isn't a bad idea to keep a lighter with you. In addition to getting a fire going, if needed, they have several other uses, such as sterilizing a needle to pop a blister, melting the freshly cut end of a length of rope to keep it from fraying, and being a backup source of light.

I don't recommend going with one of the cheap disposables you'll find in baskets near gas station cash registers. They leak and are prone to breakage. Pay the tiny bit extra for a name brand, such as Bic. Personally, I favor the Exotac titanLIGHT.

In most city environments, finding tinder will probably be easy. There always seems to be some kind of paper and such nearby. However, hedge your bet and put some homemade or store-bought tinder in your EDC bag, just in case.

## PRY BAR

This one is even more of a stretch than a multitool for most people, but it is still worth mentioning. In recent years, pocket-size pry bars have becoming increasingly common among preppers and survivalists. They're used for everything from opening wooden shipping crates to slicing open cardboard boxes to prying open stubborn doors and windows.

I see them as something of a bridge between a knife and a multitool. Some pry bars have attachment points for screwdriver bits, which gives the tool a larger range of use. If you feel the pry bar is something that fits in your wheelhouse, concentrate on finding one that's large enough to actually be useful while still being comfortable to carry.

## PERSONAL PROTECTIVE EQUIPMENT (PPE)

One of the memories from the 9/11 attacks that stands out to me even this many years later is seeing the crowds of people fleeing the area on foot, covered head to toe in dust. Of course, there is any number of other reasons why some types of PPE would be handy to have with you, including having to negotiate your way past or through a construction zone.

Masks have become commonplace throughout the world, courtesy of COVID-19. Even if you're not required to wear them in your area, it is still a good idea to have a couple of them stashed in your EDC bag.

Protective eyewear is another item that you might consider keeping around. It need not be anything expensive or fancy. An old pair of swimming goggles will be enough in most cases. The idea in certain situations is to give you something to keep your vision clear if there's a lot of dust or smoke in the air.

One more suggestion is a pair of gloves. Not nitrile or latex, something a little more solid, such as leather. You may never need to use them, but if you end up in an area filled with debris or something, you'll be glad you have them.

## SELF-DEFENSE

While the choice of what to carry for your protection is an intensely personal one, it most definitely should be part of your EDC. If you carry a firearm, spare ammunition should also be part of the equation.

The weapon should not be buried in the bottom of a bag or pack. Instead it should be readily accessible. Not only that, but you should regularly practice pulling the weapon so that it becomes a matter of muscle memory.

## OFF-BODY EDC

The point to having the off-body EDC is to have the ability to carry more than you can comfortably fit in your pockets, and have it packed in a container that you can keep close at hand throughout your day. For women, the old standby has been the purse. For guys, well, call it a man purse if you must.

Here are a few things to consider putting into your bag or pack.

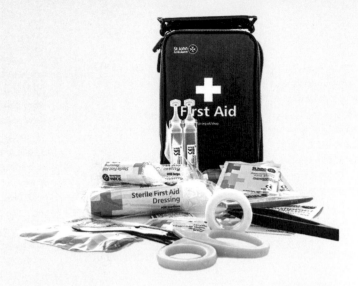

## FIRST-AID KIT

A small first aid kit can be really handy. Nothing elaborate, just some of the basics that will allow you to handle routine injuries. Suggestions include:

- Adhesive bandages

- Antiseptic ointment

- Gauze pads

- Pain relievers

- OTC meds for upset stomach

- Tape

- Tweezers

- Magnifying glass

- Nitrile gloves

You could go a step further and purchase or put together what's called a blowout kit. This is different than the average first aid kit in that the main purpose is to handle traumatic injuries, such as gunshot wounds. It should have:

- Tourniquet

- Hemostatic agent

- Compression dressing

- Paramedic shears

- Sharpie marker

That last one is for writing the time you applied the tourniquet and/ or hemostatic agent. Write this directly on the person's body. If you're going to carry a firearm for defense, you absolutely should carry what's necessary to treat a gunshot wound.

## TOOL KIT

This is another component that's best suited for a bag or pack, but it can be handy in many situations, particularly in an urban environment. There are a variety of small pouches or tins that can be used to house this type of kit, keeping it all organized in your bag until you need it. Here is what I recommend keeping in a tool kit:

- Small adjustable wrench

- Hex bit driver with various bits

- Mini screwdrivers

- Kevlar cordage

- Several feet of duct tape wrapped on a pencil stub

- Sewing needles

- Black thread wrapped on a bobbin

For the cordage, shop for "Kevlar kite string" because it tends to be the cheapest option. It is incredibly strong and can even be used to saw through PVC and similar materials.

You won't be able to do major repair work with a kit like this, but you'll be able to get many quick jobs done without needing to carry a full toolbox.

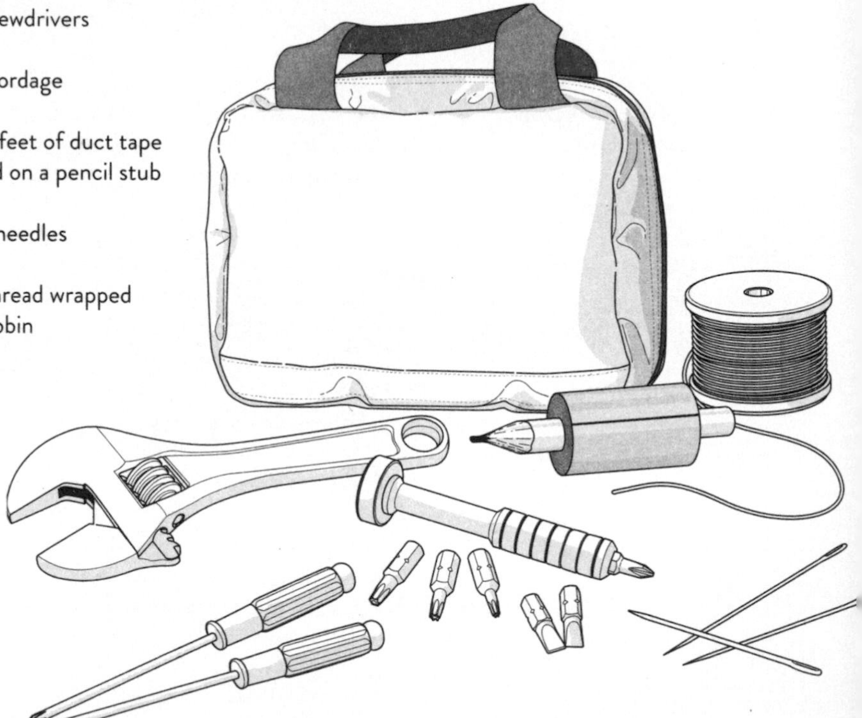

## SILLCOCK KEY

Since we're concentrating on survival and preparedness in urban areas, this handy little tool could be truly beneficial in some circumstances. Many commercial buildings have an exterior spigot, used for cleaning sidewalks, watering plants, and other such chores. However, it is often missing a handle, to prevent theft or vandalism. A sillcock key is what's used to turn that spigot on and off.

You can purchase one at just about any big box hardware store, as well as online. They come in a couple of different styles, so opt for the four-way type, just to expand your options. A sillcock key can weigh around 5 or 6 ounces and is just bulky enough to not be easily carried in your pocket with your other EDC essentials, thus making it a prime candidate for off-body carry.

While it might be considered theft to open a spigot and fill your water container, in a true crisis it is something the authorities would probably let slide.

## WATER FILTER

While we're talking about hydration, keeping a small filter, such as a Sawyer Mini, in your EDC bag is just common sense. It isn't just a matter of dealing with water from questionable sources, such as a creek flowing through a suburban park, either. Even water flowing from a city faucet could be trouble. If you don't have a way to purchase bottled water, being able to filter what's coming from the faucet is a good plan.

That said, if you have room in the bag and it isn't getting too heavy to carry, consider adding one or two bottles of water. Alternatively, you could combine the two and use a GRAYL Geopress or similar product that provides a portable water container with an integral filtration system.

## SHEMAGH

Once upon a time, a handkerchief or bandana of some kind was found in just about every guy's back pocket. It was a common as pocket lint. Today, they aren't nearly as ubiquitous. What I recommend is going a step beyond the usual snot rag anyway, and picking up a shemagh to keep in your EDC bag. The shemagh is a traditional head covering found in the Middle East, kind of like a cross between a bandana and a scarf. They've become popular around the world due to their versatility. It is a square piece of cloth, typically measuring between 40 and 48 inches (100 x 120 cm) on a side. Usually made of cotton or sometimes a cotton blend, they come in a huge range of colors and patterns. I would suggest choosing something earthy so as to avoid accidentally ending up with a color that could get you in trouble in the wrong part of town, marking you as being affiliated with a gang.

There are a ton of uses for the shemagh that go well beyond keeping the sun off your head.

- In cold weather, it can serve as a scarf around your neck.

- It can be a face covering to help prevent inhalation of smoke or dust.

- In hot weather, it can be used to mop sweat from your face and neck.

- Soak it in water and drape it over your neck to cool down.

- It can be an improvised bandage.

- Ball it up to use as a pillow on a long bus ride.

They weigh nearly nothing and while one will add a little bulk to your bag, you could use it to cushion other items while you travel.

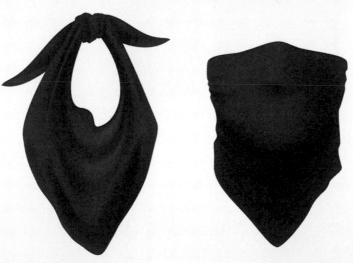

# CHAPTER 8

# HOME SAFETY

**PREPPING MEANS BEING READY TO HANDLE A WIDE RANGE OF EMERGENCIES. THIS INCLUDES PROTECTING YOUR HOME AGAINST FIRE AND OTHER HAZARDS. WHILE THIS STUFF MIGHT NOT BE AS EXCITING AS, SAY, BUILDING A BUG-OUT BAG OR SPENDING A DAY AT THE GUN RANGE, THESE MUNDANE KINDS OF EMERGENCIES ARE MORE LIKELY TO OCCUR THAN A MASS INVASION OF SOME FOREIGN ENTITY BENT ON YOUR COMPLETE DESTRUCTION.**

## HOUSE FIRES

From 2015 to 2019, US firefighters responded to an astounding average of 346,800 home structure fires each year, according to the National Fire Protection Association. Cooking was the leading cause for these fires, although smoking was the leading cause for fires that resulted in deaths.

As unfortunately common as they are, they highlight the importance of making your home is equipped to handle the risk of fire.

## SMOKE DETECTORS

You should have at least one on every level of your home. The National Fire Protection Association takes it further and recommends there also should be one smoke alarm in each bedroom. There are two ways these devices detect fire. Photoelectric sensors will detect visible fire particles, where ionization-sensing ones will alert on particles that aren't visible. Look for models that incorporate both types of technology. A bright LED light is also nice, because it can help your family find their way out in the dark.

## CARBON MONOXIDE DETECTOR

While they look a lot alike, the carbon monoxide (CO) detector and the smoke detector work very differently and protect against distinctly different threats. CO is an odorless, colorless gas that can kill. Each floor in the home should have a CO detector. It should be installed on the ceiling or on a wall at least 5 feet (150 cm) up from the floor. Don't install it near a fireplace or any other flame-producing device.

# FLASHLIGHTS

Because you never know where you might be when the power fails and the lights go out, it is a good idea to have at least one flashlight stashed in each room around the home. These don't all need to be high-end, superbright models. Just something that will keep you from banging your shins on the coffee table as you make your way through the home.

If you have children, opt for a dynamo (crank-powered) flashlight for their rooms. Kids being kids, you know they will be playing with the light. This way, you don't have to worry about a dead battery.

Stress to the children that the flashlight should be put back where it came from when they're done playing with it, so you'll be able to find it quickly if needed.

## FIRE EXTINGUISHER

All extinguishers are not made equal. They are formulated to handle different types of fire and are differentiated by class.

CLASS A: Wood, paper, and other ordinary combustible material.

CLASS B: Flammable liquids such as oil and alcohol.

CLASS C: Electrical equipment.

CLASS D: Combustible metals, such a magnesium or lithium.

CLASS K: Typically for commercial kitchens, used on cooking fires.

For most homes, a standard ABC extinguisher will be enough. While logic dictates to keep one in the kitchen, that's actually not a wise idea. While yes, that's where there's a greater risk of fire breaking out, that also means you might not be able to easily reach the extinguisher. Keep it in a room

# ALARM
## TESTING

All alarms, including smoke detectors, should be tested at least every six months. Swap the batteries for fresh ones and make sure the alarm is loud enough to be heard throughout the home.

Also, make sure you can tell the difference between the sound of the smoke alarm and the carbon monoxide alarm, so you know how to respond when you hear one of them.

adjacent to the kitchen. The garage is another good location for one.

While they don't truly expire, most models aren't at their best beyond 10 to 15 years. Use a permanent marker to write on the extinguisher the date you purchased it and plan to replace it in about 10 years. Check the user's manual for testing instructions and follow them at least monthly, if not weekly, to ensure the extinguisher will work when you need it.

In the event of an actual fire, remember the acronym **PASS**.

**PULL** the safety pin.

**AIM** the nozzle or hose at the base of the fire.

**SQUEEZE** the lever or trigger.

**SWEEP** the nozzle or hose from side to side.

No matter what, never throw water on a grease or oil fire. Doing so will accomplish nothing other than spreading those flames farther.

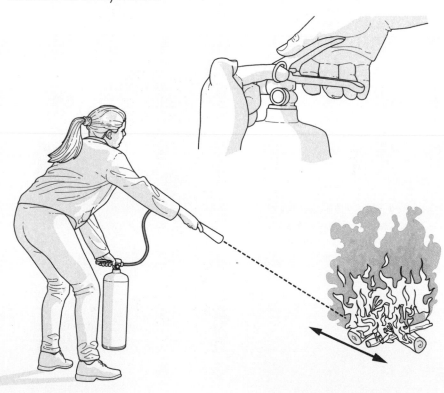

## UTILITY SHUTOFFS

Virtually every urban residential building will utilize municipal water services and natural gas. It is important that you know where the shut-off valves are located and how to use them. If you rent a house, the landlord should show you where these valves are found. Apartment and condominium buildings might have individual valves for each unit, or just one for the building.

## WATER

If you're working on what should be a quick plumbing upgrade, such as installing a new faucet, and things go awry, knowing where the shut-off valve to stop the flow of water will be helpful. There could be individual shut-off valves near each fixture, such as a sink or toilet. However, some properties rely on a single main shut-off valve. Take a look around your property so you know where these are in an emergency. The main shut-off valve is often located near the water heater.

If you need to drain the water from the pipes, open the faucet at the highest point in the home, then continue through the rest of the home to let the water flow out.

# DRYER
## FIRES

According to the Red Cross, 9 out of 10 appliance fires involve the clothes dryer. Many of these could be prevented by simply cleaning the lint trap after each use. Don't let it pile up. It takes just a second to swipe it clean. Toss the lint in the trash or save some of it to use as tinder for your next backyard fire.

## GAS

If you smell gas, hear gas escaping, or suspect a break in the gas line, shutting off the valve might be a good idea until a professional arrives to inspect the situation. There are two valves, one outside the home and one inside. The one outside is at your gas meter, which should be easy enough to locate. You can find the inside valve by following the pipe that enters the home from the meter. You should use the inside valve unless for some reason it is inaccessible.

The valve will look like a lever. All you need to do is turn it so it is perpendicular to the pipe it is installed on. While you can purchase a gas wrench for this purpose, an adjustable wrench will also do the job. I recommend keeping a wrench near the valve to save time searching for one in an emergency.

No matter your reason for shutting it off, it must only be turned on again by someone from the gas company.

## HOUSEHOLD CHEMICALS

Most homes have a large collection of cleansers and other products that, if used or stored incorrectly, can be hazardous. They might make our lives easier by loosening and removing soap scum, but they can do more harm than good if you're not careful with them.

### READ LABELS

We often skip this step, assuming we know all we need to know about the product, which can be detrimental to our safety. Read the entire label, including directions for use as well as any and all warnings. If you see something you don't understand, either don't use the product or do more research.

### DON'T SWAP CONTAINERS

Keep the product in its original container if at all possible. However, there are some chemicals that are sold in a condensed form, where it must be mixed with water or something else before use. In those cases, use a container dedicated to that mixture and label it prominently.

### USE PERSONAL PROTECTIVE EQUIPMENT

While you probably don't need a hazmat suit to mop your floor, it is wise to wear eye protection and gloves when using chemical products, such as when scrubbing bathtubs and showers. Getting some of that cleanser splashed in your eye won't do much to improve your day.

### STORE PROPERLY

Don't keep chemicals in the same cabinet as your food or water. Never use your cookware or dishes to mix or store chemical products. Make sure that young children cannot access the products, too. Keep those cabinets locked when you're not using them.

### BLEACH + AMMONIA= BAD NEWS

Adding these two cleaning agents together creates chloramine gas, which can be deadly. This is one reason why it is so important to read labels before using cleaning products. Sometimes products have one or the other of these as ingredients and you might unknowingly create a bad situation by mixing them.

## TRIPPING HAZARDS

This is one of the most common causes of injury in the home, especially for the elderly. Many accidents end up causing serious injury, even death. My maternal grandmother was visiting friends when she tripped on a slightly uneven concrete landing outside the home, falling backward and striking her head. The head injury she sustained led to her death a few months later.

Here are some ways you can reduce the risk of slipping or falling.

### KEEP WALKWAYS CLEAR.

This means making sure you don't have extension cords going across the floor, where you could stumble on them, as well as securing rugs and carpets so they don't bunch up or slide under your feet. Furniture should be positioned so that you don't have to navigate a maze to get from one side of the room to the other, especially in the dark during a power outage.

### AVOID SLIPPERY FLOORS.

The bottom of the bathtub should have some degree of traction. Add nonslip strips if needed. Use rugs in the bathroom that have nonskid bottoms so you're not stepping on a wet floor when you get out of the shower or tub. If appropriate, install grab bars in the shower and near the toilet.

### EXAMINE THE STAIRS.

How often do we end up walking up or down stairs with our arms full, such as when carrying laundry, and thus we're not able to see where we're stepping? If you have staircases in the home, take a close look at them. If the carpet is loose, have it fixed. Don't leave things on the stairs, such as shoes or magazines. Make sure you keep the entire stairway clear at all times.

### INSTALL PROPER LIGHTING.

It is far easier to avoid tripping hazards if you can see them. Have good lighting along all exterior walkways, steps, and near entrances to the home.

### TAKE CARE OF ICE AND SNOW.

If possible, clear a wide path from your front door to your vehicle and use salt or other products to melt ice. If you're unable to handle this work yourself, find someone reliable who can do it. Believe it or not, there are still young adults out there who are willing to break a sweat for a little cash. Consider using grip tape or some other kind of device to improve traction on exterior steps in bad weather.

# CHAPTER 9

# FINANCES

**ONE OF THE WORST PARTS ABOUT BEING BROKE IS THAT WHAT MIGHT BE A SMALL INCONVENIENCE FOR ANOTHER FAMILY IS A MAJOR CRISIS FOR YOU. LET'S SAY YOUR CAR BREAKS DOWN AND IT WILL COST $300 TO GET IT BACK ON THE ROAD. WITHOUT THIS CAR, YOU CAN'T GET TO WORK.**

If you're not in a good place financially, coming up with that money won't be easy, especially in a hurry. It may mean you can't buy groceries that week, plus you may be late on your credit card payment. That, in turn, means you'll be charged a late fee and incur a ding on your credit score. Not to mention the stress and anxiety you'll experience throughout this situation.

While financial health isn't as exciting as building up your food storage or learning marksmanship with a new firearm, it is one of the most important elements in your overall preparedness plan. There are several components to this:

- Reduce debt

- Increase income

- Establish an emergency fund

- Insurance

- Estate planning

These work together to keep your head well above water.

## REDUCE DEBT

This is one of the first steps you should take toward financial independence. Every dollar that goes out toward bills is one less dollar you can spend on what you truly want, right? However, debt reduction isn't easy. It requires discipline, sacrifice, and hard work, all of which is why many people struggle with it.

One of the most common mistakes people make is to hope and pray for some massive windfall that will wipe the slate clean, such as a lottery win or an inheritance from a heretofore unknown rich uncle. The sad fact is that the real world doesn't typically work this way.

There are various approaches to paying off bills, but this is one that I know from personal experience works. Start by making a list of all of your revolving credit accounts. These are your credit cards and store charge accounts. Note the current balance due for each of them. Call the customer service number for each account and ask them if there is anything they can do to help you retire the debt quicker, such as temporarily reducing the interest rate. You might be surprised at how many are willing to work with you on this.

Then, take another look at the list and pick out the account that has the smallest balance. Each month,

# WORK
## THE SYSTEM

My wife, without a doubt, is a financial genius. Here's just one example of her prowess. Some years ago, she found a credit card that offered an annual cash-back bonus, based on how much the card was used. Over time, one by one, she set up our monthly bills to run through that credit card. Utilities, mortgage, health insurance premiums, auto insurance premiums, all of those and more. We also use this card for almost every routine expense, from groceries to gas for our vehicles.

Each month, the balance is paid in full so that we don't incur interest charges. We're not spending any more money than we normally would, we're just running it all through this one card. As a result, we've racked up several hundred dollars in cash-back bonuses, which is essentially free money.

This particular approach isn't for the faint of heart. It takes tremendous discipline and willpower. But if you're able to make it work, the rewards are pretty decent.

pay as much as you can possibly afford on that bill, while still paying the minimum due on everything else so you don't fall behind. Once that debt is paid in full, take what you were paying on it and add it to the minimum on the next lowest balance bill. Over time, provided you don't add much in the way of new charges, you'll be able to dig your way out of the hole.

This approach is sometimes referred to as the "debt snowball". I'm hardly the first person to come up with it. My parents were doing it back in the early 1980s.

As you go along, watch for other ways you can speed up the debt reduction process. For example, some credit card companies will periodically send out ads for balance transfers, offering exceptionally low interest rates for a specified period of time, such as a year or 18 months. This might be worth exploring, if you feel you'll be able to pay it off in full within the given time frame. However, read the details carefully. With some of them, if you don't repay the balance in full within the given time frame, you'll get slammed with additional interest charges, which defeats the whole purpose.

## INCREASE INCOME
If you're able to bring in a few extra bucks here and there, it'll give you a little more breathing room, whether you're using the funds to pay off bills, finance your prepping, or just stashing it away for emergencies. As with debt reduction, don't concentrate on finding some way to bring in several hundred dollars extra each month, because that's not realistic for most people. Instead, seek ways you can bring in a little at a time on a steady basis.

One way is to monetize a hobby. If you're a gardener, maybe you can make a few dollars selling seedlings in the spring and excess produce in the fall. Who knows, it might really take off and you could end up getting a regular stand at a local farm market.

If you lack the yard space for something like that, you might be able to set up a table or two indoors to do seedlings each spring that you can then sell to neighbors who do have small gardens. Play your cards right and maybe you can even barter for some of the resulting produce when it is harvested.

If you're mechanically inclined, you might be able to set up a side gig repairing lawn mowers, snow blowers, and similar equipment. You could even go so far as to offer to take care of basic lawn maintenance for a reasonable price. This might be particularly

LOCAL, IN SEASON          £/Kg £/lb          INSIDE THE SHOP          £/Kg £/lb

SQUASH FROM THE WALL
SPROUTS £1.00
CELERIAC /kg
SAVOY CABBAGE
RED CABBAGE
CAULIFLOWER
COURGETTES
PURPLE SPROUTING
ROMANESCO
SWEDE /kg

MIXED SALAD BABY LEAVES
CHERRY VINE TOMATOES
BELL PEPPERS
MUSHROOMS (CLOSED CAP)
LEMONS/LIMES
ICEBERG LETTUCE
CUCUMBERS
CELERY HEAD
SPRING ONIONS

well received in areas that have a large number of senior citizens.

Spinning out of that, how about doing odd jobs for people in the community, such as cleaning gutters, pressure-washing patios, or doing small repair jobs around the house? Don't offer services you can't perform well, of course, but sometimes all that's needed is just a little elbow grease.

Making and selling craft items can be lucrative, if you find the right niche. I know one person who was making a decent amount of extra money rehabbing old furniture items at rummage sales and even objects that had been set out by the curb as trash. She'd fix what was broken, slap on a coat of paint, and turn a tidy profit.

I know someone else who, prior to the COVID pandemic, was making good money working in her kitchen. About once a month or so, she'd whip up a big pot of homemade soup or a batch of tamales and sell it off to friends and family. It didn't take long for her to establish a sizeable list of regular customers, because the food was excellent and reasonably priced and you don't need a lot of storage space for something on this scale. Just buy your supplies as needed for each bulk meal you cook.

When the pandemic lockdowns started going into effect, one

# THE IMPORTANCE
## OF FUN

Years ago, when our children were young, we went through a particularly rough financial patch that lasted a few years. It was stressful and just plain ugly. Our combined annual household income was about $12,000 and our mortgage payment was about $1,000 a month. When I say we were broke, I'm talking we barely had two nickels to rub together. It was a constant balancing act just to put food on the table and keep a roof over our heads.

Yet even so, we felt it was imperative that we worked at having fun as often as possible. We found free things to do with the kids, such a simply going to a park to play for a few hours or making up games to play at home. Any time we had a little extra money come in, I made sure we took just a little to splurge on something fun. For example, if we had a rummage sale, I'd take ten bucks to rent a movie and get a pizza.

Financial stress is horrible, but you can find ways to still blow off a little steam for free.

enterprising young man in my area started a delivery service. While many people could order takeout food from restaurants, he took things a step further. He would pick up and deliver just about anything you ordered, from beer to cigarettes, doughnuts to diapers.

This is just one more example of someone who saw a need and found a way to earn an income filling it.

## ONLINE ACCESS

Even if you don't normally do your bill paying online, take the time to set up online access to every account that offers it. Utilities, credit cards, banking, everything. In the event of a disaster, particularly one that requires you to evacuate from home for a length of time, you'll still be able to access your money and make payments as needed remotely, using either the various websites or apps you've downloaded to your phone.

While we might expect that companies will work with us in the wake of a crisis, the fact is that they're not necessarily required to do so. As we often say, plan for the worst and hope for the best.

## PASSWORDS

We live in a world dominated by passwords. They're needed for everything, from accessing our e-mail to being able to watch our favorite streaming services. If you want to generate a truly secure password, avoid:

- Names and nicknames (you, family members, pets)

- Birth dates

- Social security numbers

- Phone numbers (home or cell)

- Addresses

- Vehicles

All of that information is relatively easy to learn and could be used to crack your password.

A better approach is to generate a random string of letters, numbers, and symbols. Of course, the more complex the password is, the more difficult it can be to remember. Here's one approach that might work for you.

Start with a favorite book or song, something you can easily recall. We'll use a nursery rhyme as an example. Look at the first line:

Old MacDonald had a farm, E-I-E-I-O.

Take the first letter of each word, capitalizing every other one:

OmHaFelelo

Then, add a 4-, 5-, or 6-digit number that has some significance to you. Maybe your locker combination from work or the gym, for example:

OmHaFelelo102217

Lastly, add in a couple of symbols.

!OmHaFelelo+102217*

A password such as this would be very difficult to crack, yet should be easy enough to remember, especially after you've used it a few times.

## ESTABLISH AN EMERGENCY FUND

Reducing your debt and increasing your income will both help you to free up funds to set aside for emergencies. It is important to understand that this emergency fund is to be used only when absolutely necessary. It isn't money you're putting away toward a vacation or a new rifle. This is strictly for situations where the financial need is critical and you have no other options.

One of the most common reasons a family will need to dip into such an account is due to unexpected job loss. Long gone are the days when you could be employed by a company and expect to stay there for the next 30 years until retirement. In today's climate, just making it to the next paycheck can feel like an accomplishment.

The initial goal should be to set aside enough money to pay all of your normal bills and expenses for one full month. Don't stop there, of course. Keep building it a little at a time with every paycheck. You might be surprised how quickly it'll start to add up.

## CASH ON HAND

As part of your emergency fund, be sure to keep at least some amount of cash readily available. There are a few reasons for this. For starters, cash is king when it comes to negotiations. If you come across a great potential bargain on something, such as at a rummage sale, having cash on hand might seal the deal.

One thing many people learned during the COVID lockdowns in 2020 was that getting money out of the bank isn't always easy. In some cases, there might be delays due to limited hours or staff at your local branch.

If there is a major power outage or sustained Internet issues, you might have trouble making purchases using a credit or debit card. In those situations, it'll only be cash. On top of that, in the event of a sudden evacuation, you might not have the time to run to the ATM and make a withdrawal.

My suggestion is to keep at least enough cash on hand for:

• One full tank of gas

- One or two nights at a cheap but decent motel

- Meals on the road for a couple of days.

Add another $100 or so for incidentals, if possible. Keep this money somewhere that you can access it easily, but that isn't too vulnerable to discovery and theft. A good quality home safe is great, but if you don't have that as an option, look for other hiding places, such as in a photo album stuffed on a closet shelf.

## INSURANCE

As part of your overall financial planning, you should speak to an insurance agent about policies to protect your home and property. While house insurance is typically a requirement when taking out a mortgage, even those who rent should take this step.

Talk to your agent about any specific coverages you feel you might need, such as protection for extensive collections of items that are either valuable or difficult to replace, such as jewelry or firearms. Keep in mind that each piece adds to the total. For example, while none of your books might be especially valuable (in a fiscal sense – many will, of course, be invaluable), if you have several hundred of them, even if you value

them each at just a few dollars, that will add up quickly.

Make it a semi-annual event to spend an afternoon going through your entire home with a camera and recording video footage in each room. Narrate it as you go along, detailing all of the items being shown. Open drawers and closets so you don't overlook anything. Take particular note of model numbers, serial numbers, and other identifiers. This will help zero in on replacement value for any insurance claims.

It doesn't matter if the rooms aren't tidy and spotlessly clean, that's not the point. What you're doing is documenting your possessions so that they can be recovered if they're stolen or replaced if they are destroyed. Keep this footage on password-protected thumb drives. Store at least one offsite somewhere safe. When I worked outside the home, I kept one locked in my office desk. If that's not a workable option for you, perhaps you could consider storing one with a trusted friend or relative.

While you're at it, look in to getting life insurance policies. It is an unfortunate reality that burial, cremation, and funeral costs are expensive. Which conveniently leads right into the next section of our discussion.

## ESTATE PLANNING

One more element in the financial realm is planning for your ultimate demise. Let's face facts – nobody gets out of life alive. I speak from experience here. My father passed in 2019 and, while he had a will in place, it was sparse. Not only that, but he had no life insurance, no savings, no funds set aside at all. Between funeral expenses, home repairs to get the house ready to sell, fees for disposing of the things nobody wanted, and storage fees for the stuff we did want to keep, my wife and I spent tens of thousands of dollars out of our pockets.

Don't leave a mess like this for your loved ones. Doing so robs them of the time to grieve and mourn. Speak to an attorney and set up plans for your last wishes as well as a living will and similar documents. It is important, of course, that responsible family members know where to find those plans.

Part of this area of financial planning is to make sure everyone knows what to do when a death occurs. You might go so far as to write up a checklist of sorts and make sure everyone knows where to find it. As most people who've gone through the sudden death of a family member will tell you, it can be difficult to concentrate and think things through. Having a short list of instructions will make things easier.

The first thing that should happen is to notify the authorities. The death needs to be officially recorded and the body removed. In many situations, this will be a call to the emergency services.

Someone will also need to contact the funeral home to start the process with them, which will include taking custody of the body. At some point, they should ask you about the death certificate, specifically how many certified copies you'll want. These certificates are needed to prove the death to creditors and most of them won't accept photocopies or scans. They will require originals. This means you'll want several of them –at least ten.

The deceased's attorney, financial adviser, and/or insurance agent should be notified right away. Each may have specific instructions for you as well as forms that will need to be completed.

Notify their employer as well. This isn't just so they know the position will need to be filled but because some employers provide death benefits to the family.

Cancel all streaming, Internet, phone and television subscriptions. What can make this process much easier is to put a dedicated family member on the account ahead of time. This way, they can initiate

# LIVING TRUST & ESTATE PLANNING

the cancellation process without incurring any delay.

Call each of the person's creditors and begin the process of either canceling the accounts (in the case of credit cards and similar accounts) or switching them over to someone appropriate (utility companies, for example). You may find that some of these accounts have insurance coverage, at least of a sort, that allows for a grace period before balances need to be paid.

On a similar note, contact the three major credit bureaus (TransUnion, Equifax, Experian) and notify them of the death. This will help to curtail any subsequent fraud or identity theft.

Remember, prepping should involve day-to-day planning as well as mitigating risks for major crises. Some people tend to overlook the financial side of things, because they're counting on a societal collapse occurring at some point in the future. The reality is that by ignoring the importance of smart money handling, all you're doing is ensuring that a personal emergency is guaranteed to happen and probably soon.

# CHAPTER 10
# SOFT SKILLS

**WHEN WE TALK ABOUT SURVIVAL PLANNING, WE TEND TO FOCUS ON WHAT WE MIGHT CALL HARD SKILLS, SUCH AS FIRE STARTING, TRACKING, FOOD PRESERVATION, EVEN COOKING. BECAUSE THEY AREN'T AS DYNAMIC OR VISIBLE, WE OFTEN FORGET ABOUT THE FLIP SIDE OF THE COIN – THE SOFT SKILLS.**

There are various ways to look at the difference between the two, but it basically boils down to: hard skills typically offer measurable results, whereas soft skills are more along the lines of personality traits, albeit ones that you can learn and hone with practice. Another way to look at it is that soft skills aren't specific to a single job or task, while hard skills are focused on accomplishing a certain goal or reaching an objective.

In the prepper arena, there are several sets of soft skills that are particularly helpful. The bonus is that they are useful in your normal day-to-day life as well, especially if you don't live a solitary life and have to interact with a number of other people regularly.

## INTERPERSONAL COMMUNICATION

Most people would agree, given a little thought, that communication is one of the biggest problems in our society. To put it more precisely, it is the lack of proper communication that's the issue. Think about arguments you've experienced in just the last couple of weeks. How many of them stemmed from an initial miscommunication?

Being able to share your thoughts in such a way that is easily understood by others is, indeed, a rare skill these days, or at least that's how it seems. In a crisis, when emotions are already running high, it can be critical to avoid adding to the stress by ensuring conversations are as drama-free as possible. That means communicating efficiently and effectively.

## ACTIVE LISTENING

This is probably the single-most important aspect of good communication. Far too often, when we're in a discussion, we're focused on what we're going to say next instead of truly listening to what someone is telling us.

Active listening operates on a couple of different levels. First, it works to clarify what has been said and ensures proper understanding. Second, it slows the conversation down a little, which allows for a little breathing room, which is important if things are getting heated.

It works like this. You listen to the other person, then repeat back to him or her what you understood them to say, in your own words. The goal is to clear up any misunderstanding, anything that might be lost in translation. You don't do this with every sentence they utter. Instead, you just check in at various points in

# TWO IMPORTANT WORDS

There is a two-word phrase that will go a long way toward defusing arguments before they spiral out of control, especially between spouses or others who are exceptionally close. No, the words aren't, "I'm sorry." That's uttered entirely too often without sincerity.

No, the phrase is, "I understand."

This small phrase shows you are acknowledging their point of view. You aren't agreeing with everything they're saying; you're just indicating that you understand what they're telling you. Honestly, that's what we often want more than anything else, just for the other person to recognize our perspective.

the conversation, paraphrasing or summarizing what you've heard, asking if you're correct with your understanding. That last part is important, because it gives him or her the chance to correct you if needed.

## KEEP IT SHORT

One of the fastest ways to lose someone's attention in a discussion is to chase down one rabbit hole after another, constantly straying from the topic on hand. If you're trying to communicate important information, keep it succinct and to the point. Stick to the facts and save the commentary and editorializing for later.

## PROVIDE FEEDBACK

The more people talk, the more information they provide, sometimes without realizing it. Show you're listening by giving something back to the conversation. Nod your head, for example. It will keep them engaged, because nobody wants to talk to a brick wall.

Another aspect of providing feedback is to ask appropriate questions here and there, especially about minor details. This is a great way to keep the conversation moving, which is the entire point if you're on a fact-finding mission of some kind.

## LEADERSHIP

Here's the thing. An awful lot of people think they are born leaders, but they aren't. True leadership has little to do with being the best in a group and everything to do with working to make every person in the group better.

Leading a group also involves using the available skills and resources efficiently. This means the leader has to have a good handle on each person's strengths and weaknesses, as well as understand group dynamics.

While leaders do have to make difficult decisions, sometimes in an instant, that doesn't mean they have to lack compassion and empathy. In other words, the most effective leaders are those who can see and understand the different perspectives but still do what it takes to move the group forward.

## CONFLICT RESOLUTION

Some may consider this a subset of interpersonal communication, but it is important enough to warrant a separate entry on the list. If members of your family or group are constantly bickering, not much will get accomplished. Being able to resolve conflicts will also go far in improving morale, because few people truly enjoy being in a contentious environment.

There are several strategies that can be used, depending on the situation and the people involved.

## CONCESSION

Here, you're basically just acknowledging that the argument isn't worth your time or energy. You surrender your point and move on with your life. Many online disputes fall into this category. If giving up does you no harm, this may be the approach you'll want to use.

## COMPROMISE

We do this all the time, right? We give up a little to get a little, meeting in the middle. However, if this approach is used too often, it can lead to anger or resentment, because those involved may feel as though they never truly get what they want. That said, it is an excellent option if there's a stalemate. If nothing else, exploring a compromise can sometimes further open the channels of communication and lead to further discussion.

## COLLABORATION

If everyone is willing to talk it through, this is a great approach. It is one of the few true win-win strategies. However, it requires all involved to commit to finding a workable solution that benefits everyone. This is why it is probably the most difficult option to implement, because if even one person isn't on board, it will probably fail.

## MEDIATION

If you have a neutral third party available, someone who is willing to work with those involved with the conflict, it can work well. The mediator isn't a judge and doesn't make any final decisions. Instead, that person's role is simply to help guide the parties involved to come to an agreement by asking questions and keeping the lines of communication open.

## ARBITRATION

This strategy also involved a third party, but in this case that person is the decision maker. Those involved with the argument or conflict plead their cases and allow the arbiter to decide on a course of action. This only works if everyone agrees to abide by the decision.

## TIME MANAGEMENT

This can be incredibly important in the wake of a disaster. Being able to accurately determine which actions take precedence is essential. There are only so many hours in the day, and if you have a long list of chores that need to be completed, being successful will hinge upon you managing that time wisely.

Where this falls apart for some people is an inability to gauge how long a given task will probably take. They will often drastically underestimate the time involved, and, by the end of the day, will be frustrated at how little they feel was accomplished. A good way to mitigate this is to pay attention to how long it takes to do certain tasks on a regular basis. Maybe keep a log for a week or two and jot down the time spent engaging in them. Doing so will give you a basis for comparison down the road.

## CRITICAL THINKING

This is an area where many people seem to falter. Confirmation bias refers to the tendency of seeing what we want to see and looking for viewpoints that agree with our own notions, disregarding those that don't fall in line with what we believe. The thing is, we're not always right.

Just because it doesn't mesh with what you want to believe doesn't automatically make it incorrect. Think objectively and analyze the information using logic and common sense. Especially on social media, inciteful headlines tend to get passed around without much thought, simply because we want to believe they're true. All it does is add to the static and noise, without contributing anything meaningful.

While at first blush it can seem that prepping involves the acquisition of stuff more than anything else, the reality is that we should be just as heavily invested in developing our skills as we are in developing a stockpile of hard goods. These soft skills are important in times of crisis as well as just our normal daily living. If you can't get along with others now, it'll get infinitely worse when everyone is stressed out and anxious in the wake of a disaster.

# CHAPTER 11

# EMERGENCY EVACUATION

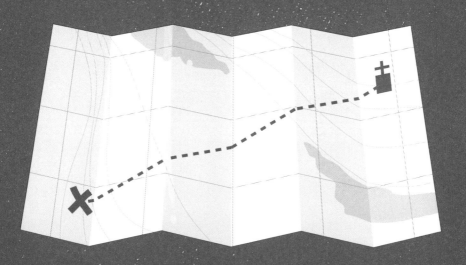

**THERE IS PERHAPS NO OTHER SUBJECT UNDER THE PREPPER UMBRELLA MORE DISCUSSED THAN EMERGENCY EVACUATION, POPULARLY REFERRED TO AS "BUGGING OUT." ONLINE FORUMS ARE RIFE WITH BUG-OUT BAG (BOB) LISTS, IDEAS FOR BUG-OUT LOCATIONS (BOLS), EVEN SUGGESTIONS FOR SETTING UP BUG-OUT TRAILERS (BOTS) AND BUG-OUT VEHICLES (BOVS). PREPPERS SURE DO LOVE ACRONYMS.**

Often, the plans shared by people involve some kind of wilderness setting, where they will live off the land, to one degree or another, because they either travel to a remote destination or resort to a nomadic existence, as portrayed in entirely too many Hollywood movies. However, the realism of such a plan is certainly up for debate.

The truth is that bugging out to the wilderness should be your last resort, not your primary plan, in most situations. Think about it. If a hurricane is eyeballing your town, the nearest state park is probably a bad place to go.

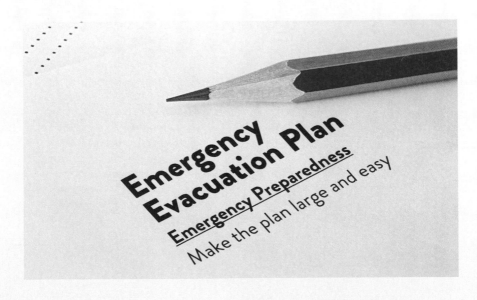

Same goes for any other natural disaster. Not to mention that if you lack the requisite skills and experience to pull it off, planning to run to the forest to live off the land is a death sentence.

In the history of the United States, every single crisis that has required some kind of evacuation has been local or, at best, regional in size. Even Hurricane Katrina, certainly one of the most devastating natural disasters to ever hit the country, was limited in scope and certainly nowhere near national level in terms of damage. In other words, assistance, food, water, shelter, and more can probably be found within a day or so of driving from the epicenter of the disaster.

That said, you absolutely should have an evacuation plan. Living in an urban area means you're surrounded by people, many of whom might be looking to beat feet in an emergency, and the last place you want to end up is on an interstate highway that has turned into a parking lot.

## WHEN TO LEAVE

The first decision you'll need to make is whether to hunker down and stay put or head out of town. As a general rule of thumb, stay home until or unless home is no longer a safe option. Odds are, home is where you have the bulk of

your emergency supplies stored. You're familiar with the area and you're probably most comfortable there. Heading out on the road exposes you to many risks, so this isn't a decision to be made lightly.

Give some thought to red flags that will push you toward loading up the car and evacuating. Some suggestions include:

- An impending disaster headed your way, such as wildfire or hurricane.

- Damage to your home that causes it to be unsafe. This could be anything from structural to just no longer being livable, such as mold developing after flood water recedes.

- Violence will probably be headed your way. This is especially a risk in dense urban areas where there will probably be high competition for limited resources.

Brainstorm other signs based on your location and the threats you're most likely to face. The idea here is to identify, well in advance, the warning signs that will indicate you need to get out of the area quickly. This will help make the decision process easier in the long run.

It is far better to jump the gun and evacuate needlessly a dozen times

than to wait too long and get stuck in the crowd the one time it is a real emergency.

## WHERE TO GO

Evacuating without a planned destination just makes you a refugee. Perhaps a well-equipped one, but a refugee nonetheless. It is in everyone's best interests that you do some homework now and determine where you can go, if the need arises. Think about it like this: If you leave it up to fate to decide where you'll go, what are the odds that you're going to like where you end up?

Ideally, you'll want to have a few options. What I suggest is having at least three places you can go, each in a different direction from home. Because we cannot know for certain what future event may result in us leaving our residence, we cannot predict the location of said event. If your bug out location is to the north, but the disaster or crisis is between you and there, then that's not necessarily going to be a viable option for you. A better plan, for example, is to have one to the north, one to the east, and one to the southwest.

Now, I know what you're thinking. No, I'm not suggesting you somehow purchase three real estate parcels or homes and outfit each of

# SCHOOLS
## AND STUDENTS

If you have school-age children, have a conversation with the administration about their emergency response plans. As a parent, you have the right to know what they will do if an evacuation order is made official. Where will you be able to retrieve your children? Work this information into your own evacuation plans.

# EMERGENCY
## SHELTERS

If at all possible, you want to avoid relying on any kind of community shelter, whether set up by local government officials, aid agencies, or even churches. These will probably be overcrowded, with extremely limited resources. The whole idea behind prepping for evacuation is to keep you from having to resort to these facilities.

Granted, they'll be better than nothing, but not by much. Plan ahead so you won't need to use them.

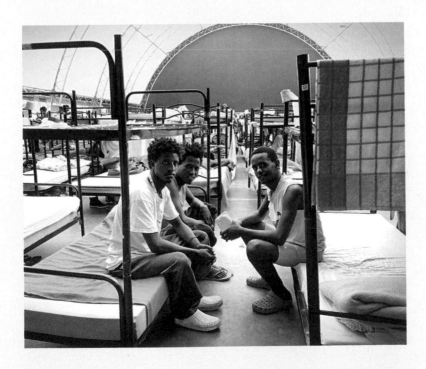

them as a survival retreat, not in the least. Instead, first think about the homes of family members and close friends where you might be able to stay for a day or two in the event of an emergency. This should involve a conversation with them, of course, along with an offer of reciprocity. Should they be the family forced out, they're welcome to stay with your family.

Another option is to look for decent, affordable motels. Again, you should be doing this ahead of time, not as you're rushing out the door. Identify one or two places that are reasonably priced and that will accommodate your needs. If you have pets, then pay particular attention to their pet policies. Contrary to popular belief, no motel in the United States is forced by law to change their rules regarding pets if there's a disaster at hand. While some might do so as an act of kindness, they're certainly not required to let Fido stay in the room if their policies dictate otherwise.

There are a couple of guidelines I recommend as you think about potential bug-out locations. First, consider distance from home. What some folks do is set up one bug-out location that's just a few miles away, another over in the next county, and a third considerably farther

# MOTELS
## AND DISASTERS

One approach I particularly endorse is to plan to stay at a motel, at least initially, to give you a roof over your head and a place you can get your breath. From there, you can explore your options once you know more about what's happening. Of course, that's also contingent upon finding a motel that has a vacancy.

What I suggest is, once you've identified two or three motels that are good options for you as an initial bug-out location, program their local, as well as corporate, reservation phone numbers into your cell phone. The moment you realize you have to leave home, start calling to make a reservation.

away. Again, the idea here is to have options from which you can select based upon the situation at the time. If your only destination is a remote cabin a few hundred miles away, there's an awful lot that can happen during such a lengthy journey, including mechanical issues as well as refueling difficulty.

With that in mind, determine how far your vehicle will go on a quarter tank of gas. For most cars, that'll be 80 to 100 miles or so. Make two assumptions:

1   You'll be driving to your bug-out location.

2   You'll have forgotten to fill the car's gas tank the day before.

Take a look at a map of your area and draw a mental circle that's about 80 miles in all directions from your home. Then start looking at bug-out location possibilities that fall inside that perimeter.

Note, however, that this is not a rule that's etched in stone. It is merely a guideline or a starting

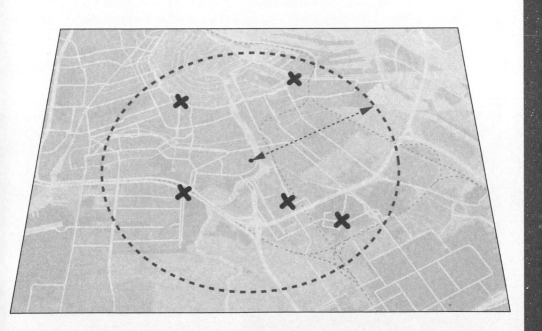

point. You're welcome to go well beyond that circle on the map. Just understand that the longer the journey takes, the more chances are that something negative might happen along the way.

## ROUTE PLANNING

Once you've identified your bug-out locations, you'll need to figure out how you're getting to them. If possible, you'll want to avoid high-traffic routes such as interstate highways. In a major evacuation, they will probably become slow-moving parking lots. A better idea is to stick to lesser traveled roads such as two-lane highways and such. Even better is if you become familiar enough with the area to know the back

roads that are typically only used by locals.

Bear in mind that authorities may institute road blocks or in some other way direct traffic along specific routes. If you can get out ahead of these actions, or avoid them by taking alternate streets, that's ideal. Again, you want to stay away from the crowd, as all they'll do is tie up the roadways and slow you down.

You can take your planning one step further and research what the government agencies in your area will do in an emergency evacuation. Contact the Emergency Management Coordinator, or whatever the equivalent for your city. If your favorite search engine

# SPLIT
## FAMILIES

When a disaster strikes, it is the absolute wrong time for egos and infighting. You need to focus on doing whatever is best for all involved, which is getting everyone to safety as quickly and efficiently as possible. If the family is split, such as from a divorce resulting in the kids dividing their time between homes, you need to have a conversation with them, as well as the other parent, about what to do in case of a crisis.

The best option might be that the noncustodial parent is responsible for picking the children up from school if he or she lives/works closest to them. If that's the case, the school should be aware of this contingency, so that there are no delays with them releasing the children to the parent.

In addition, there should be emergency supplies stationed at both homes, if possible. Remember, you don't know where the children may be when something happens. Better that they have what's needed, regardless of which home they're in at the time.

isn't helpful with coming up with the name and contact information for that person, start by calling the non-emergency phone number for the police department. They should be able to help guide you in your search.

What you want is a copy of the county disaster response plan. This is publicly available information. There may be a cost involved for copy fees or other administration, but, if you are lucky, they will have it posted somewhere online. It should tell you where they plan to funnel traffic flow, where they will set up blockades, and other actions they plan to take as soon as the evacuation order comes down. All of this information can help you determine the best routes for you and your family to take as you head out of town.

## WHAT TO BRING

The vaunted bug-out bag may seem to be the answer to any number of disasters. Here's where we're going to deviate a little from what's become popular prepper lore. While a completely equipped bug-out bag can be useful, it is hardly the panacea survival literature has made it out to be.

The truth of the matter is that in the vast majority of probably or common emergencies, a completely charged cell phone, a working vehicle, and cash or a credit card will get you out of trouble quicker than any backpack

full of equipment. Again, I'm not suggesting the bug-out bag has no place in your preps, just that it might not be as crucial to survival in many cases. Unless the crisis is truly staggering in scope, you'll probably be able to travel far enough in just a few hours to find a place to stay, get a hot meal, and buy any needed items you left at home.

That said, it is definitely a good idea to have some things packed up and ready to grab at a moment's notice. Depending on the nature of the emergency, you might not have

the benefit of time to leisurely go through the house and get a bag ready before you leave. In some instances, you might have no more than a few minutes to get out the door, and most of that time will be taken up by wrangling with the kids and critters.

However, think along the lines of an impromptu trip out of town to stay at a motel, instead of running off to the woods to live off the land for several days. Here's a sample packing list to consider.

- Full change of clothing for more than two days, for each family member.

- Small toiletry kit (toothbrush, toothpaste, floss, deodorant, razor, shaving cream).

- Cash and credit cards.

- Snacks – just a few things to tide you over, along with a couple of bottles of water for each person.

- Portable water filter.

- Prescription medications for each member of the family who requires them. Enough for at least a week.

- Cell phone charger with cord.

- List of important phone numbers, in case your phone is unavailable.

- Flashlight with spare batteries.

- Small first aid kit, including stomach remedies and meds for cold/flu.

You may also want a photocopy of the front and back of your identification cards, in case you forget your wallet at home in your haste to get out the door. This is also why you should always have a stash of money and a credit card in your bag.

You can hopefully split the load between a few family members, because the clothing will be bulky. If nothing else, smaller children can probably carry a pack with just their clothes. If you have time, make sure to grab their favorite stuffed animal or other comfort item.

When our kids were little, we used to keep a box in our van that had a full set of clothes for each of them. This worked great for the rare times when they'd accidentally

spill their drink in their lap, that kind of thing. It also saved space in our bags, because we didn't need to pack the clothes; we already had them set up to travel.

Store your bag or pack somewhere easily accessible, such as the closet nearest the front door. Get into the habit of unpacking it and inspecting all of the contents at least twice a year, so you can make sure everything that is supposed to be there is still packed. Replace batteries and food as needed.

If you're bugging out, the focus will probably be on speed. You need to get on the road as quickly as possible. That's why you should have a bag packed and ready to go. If you're a parent, remember back to when you were getting ready to make that run to the hospital

# FOOD
## FOR THE BUG-OUT BAG

The goal is to keep the stomach rumbles to a minimum. You don't need to pack enough ingredients to provide five-course meals for a month straight. Keep these guidelines in mind.

1 **SHELF-STABLE**: Because you'll be keeping these in a pack or bag for months at a time, you don't want anything that will turn rancid.

2 **READY TO EAT**: Since you can't know what the situation will be if the time arrives where you need to use your bug-out food, don't plan on actually cooking anything.

3 **FAMILIAR**: An emergency evacuation is the wrong time to experiment with new foods, if you can avoid doing so.

Here are a few suggestions:

• Granola bars

• Crackers

• Pouched meats (chicken, tuna)

• Dried fruit

• Nuts or trail mix

• Peanut butter

# CACHES

Contrary to what you might hear on some TV shows, the word cache is pronounced like "cash," not "cash-ay." It refers to the notion of having prepositioned supply points away from home, where you can pick up extra food and other supplies. The traditional prepper cache has been a homemade setup using a PVC tube that's filled with your goodies, then sealed and buried.

However, it is a plan rife with risks, not the least of which is completely losing the cache to accidental discovery or outright theft.

A better solution, especially for the urban prepper, is to see about renting a small storage unit on the outskirts of town or along the route to your primary bug-out location. They are secure and many are climate-controlled, so there's less danger of things freezing in winter. Given that most such units are used to store old furniture, cartons of ill-fitting clothes, and kitchen appliances of questionable usefulness, there's little danger of roving gangs looting these buildings, at least not until after they've hit much more rewarding targets.

Just make sure you'll be able to access the unit if there's a power outage. Some of these businesses use electric-powered gates to secure access.

for the birth. I'm betting that the mother-to-be wouldn't have been too happy anyone meandering through the house, hemming and hawing about what to bring while she was dealing with ever-more-uncomfortable contractions. Evacuation may involve a similar, or even greater, sense of urgency.

## EVACUATING WITH PETS

Let's get this out of the way right now. Never leave your dogs tied up outside if you have to evacuate. Doing so could be a death sentence for them, because they can't escape from things such as floods or predators. If possible, take your critters with you. For the purposes of our discussion here, we're going to concentrate on dogs and cats, because they are among the most common pets in the United States. However, much of this information is easily adapted for other animals.

As I mentioned earlier, you'll need to take pets into account when it comes to choosing potential bug-out locations, particularly motels and similar establishments. You cannot count on a desk clerk having a soft spot for kitties and deciding

to bend the rules for you. At the same time, just figuring on leaving the animals in the car overnight is also not an acceptable idea. Make sure your entire family, including the ones that can't speak for themselves, will be welcome at your destination.

You should be prepared to bring with you certain essential items for your pets.

- Food: Enough for a few days.

- Water: Enough for a few days.

- Dishes: Collapsible for food and water.

- Medications: For at least a week.

- Restraints: Leash, collar, muzzle.

- Vet record: Documentation of all current vaccinations.

Periodically, make it a point to take a photo of you with your pet(s). It will be useful if you and the animal become separated. You can use it to help identify the pet as well as prove ownership.

## PRACTICE MAKES PERFECT

Your family won't like this next part, but it's what we might call a necessary evil. Once you have your plans drawn up, whatever they are, you need to practice them. Remember doing fire drills in

school? Same concept here.

Start simple and easy. Explain to everyone in the house ahead of time what you're going to do. Then, set a timer and have everyone get their bag and get loaded into the vehicle. Make a note of the time and look for ways they could improve, such as keeping their bags in a more accessible location.

Work on improving the time it takes to get fully evacuated, including pets and their supplies, if applicable. You don't need to do the drills every week, but you should do them on a regular basis. Get to a point to where you're not warning them in advance. Instead, you're surprising them with these practice runs. They probably won't enjoy this, but nothing good comes easy, as the saying goes.

From time to time, drive the routes you've planned to your bug out locations. Get familiar with them in all seasons as well as both day time and nighttime. The visual appearance of landmarks and other scenery can change throughout the year and, when it is happening for real, you don't want to take a wrong turn.

While there are situations where evacuation makes perfect sense, don't be so eager that you potentially hamper your efforts to survive by taking the show on the road. Stay home unless it isn't safe to do so.

CHAPTER 12
# SURVIVAL
# MENTALITY

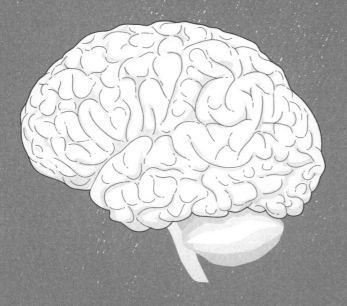

**TO BE BLUNT, IT DOESN'T MATTER HOW MUCH STUFF YOU'VE STOCKPILED, HOW MANY WEAPONS YOU'VE MASTERED, OR HOW MANY YEARS YOU'VE BEEN PREPPING. IF YOU DON'T HAVE YOUR HEAD IN THE RIGHT FRAME OF MIND, YOU'VE LOST. SURVIVAL IS FAR MORE ABOUT WHAT'S BETWEEN YOUR EARS THAN IT IS ANYTHING ELSE.**

Truth be told, your mind will make or break you. We humans are capable of incredible feats, when we put our minds to it. At the same time, your brain can be your biggest enemy. If your attitude is that you'll never be able to accomplish a given goal, you probably won't prove it right, even if you're otherwise completely capable of doing so.

Let's take a look at some of the different aspects of the survival mentality.

## BE REALISTIC

If there is a single piece of advice I could convey to you, it is this—be realistic. It is important to work on improving your skills and knowledge, of course, but it is just as critical to understand your current limitations.

If you get out of breath walking to the mailbox, planning to evacuate on foot in an emergency probably isn't the best option. Maybe once upon a time you could shoulder a 45-pound (18-kg) pack and walk for

miles and miles every day. That was probably 30 years and 95 pounds (45 kg) ago.

A common misconception among preppers and survivalists is the notion that, even though they've never so much as planted a flower before, their sealed package of heirloom seeds is all they'll need to grow enough food to feed their family if society collapses. They figure they'll just dig up the backyard, toss seeds on the ground, and then reap the bounty in a few

weeks. Unfortunately, it really doesn't work that way and even experienced gardeners would balk at such a plan.

This plays into your mindset –because, if your plans aren't realistic, then you're setting yourself up for failure. This means that when push comes to shove and the worst happens, you'll be spending your time playing catch up, instead of actually moving forward. Not to mention the blow to your morale and ego when reality slaps you in the face.

Take a hard look at your plans and make sure they are practical and realistic – given your current situation, budget, physical fitness level, and available resources. You can always adjust and modify things as you move along and improve any, or all, of those factors. But don't set yourself up for a fall by being overly ambitious about what you're truly capable of doing.

## OPTIMISM

Survivalists and preppers often get a bad rap, with constant portrayals of being focused on gloom and doom. However, I maintain that we're

# USE THE PAST
## TO SHAPE
## THE FUTURE

When the chips are down, remember that you've survived everything life has thrown at you thus far. You might be facing something larger than you've had to deal with before, but that doesn't discount the adversity you've overcome in the past. Be confident that you can handle this, too.

actually the ultimate optimists. We look at all the bad things that could happen down the road, from power outages to severe weather and more, and instead of throwing our hands up in the air and leaving it up to chance, we make preparations so that we can survive, and even thrive, in the face of adversity.

Having a positive outlook, convincing yourself right down to the core that it will all turn out okay, is a key part of the survival mindset. It can give you the energy required to do what needs to be done.

## WORK THE PROBLEM

What seems like a couple of lifetimes ago, I spent a few years working for a big box retailer. My job was primarily building bicycles and furniture displays, although I helped out in other areas from time to time. There were a few employees who spent an incredible amount of time every day complaining about just about everything. Corporate either sent too much product or not enough. There were either too many customers to get work done, or not enough customers spending money. The list went on and on.

Of course, all of this complaining accomplished exactly nothing other than taking time away from getting things done. A better plan is to take a more pragmatic approach and *work the problem*. Don't spend so much time trying to figure out the why or why not of the situation. Worry about that later. When a crisis occurs, deal with what needs to be handled in order to keep you and your family alive.

Think about it like this: If you don't get the work done, the reasons for the emergency won't matter in the slightest anyway.

## DON'T PLAN TO IMPROVISE

Preppers dearly love their hacks, their shortcuts, their improvised solutions. Make no mistake, knowing how to throw together a workable solution to a given problem from whatever's available is a priceless skill to possess. However, the entire point of preparedness is to do what you can to ensure you have on hand what you need when you need it. Don't hinder your efforts by investing a ton of time and energy into stockpiling half-baked, gimmicky ways to get the job done.

Here's an example. Several years ago, people began posting on social media that you can use crayons as improvised candles. This could be handy knowledge to have, especially if you have children and thus an excess of crayons kicking around the house. However, I've lost count

of the number of people who commented on those posts that they were going to pick up a box of crayons at the store to keep for emergencies. If you're at the store, just buy candles.

- Knowledge is knowing that crayons are wax and that wax will burn.

- Wisdom is understanding that crayons make poor candle substitutes.

- Prepping is investing in flashlights, lanterns, chemlights, candles, and other means of illumination so you don't need to burn your child's Crayolas.

If you hinge your survival plans on improvisation, you're potentially handicapping yourself from the outset. This will probably lead to frustration and anger, neither of which are beneficial in a crisis. Learn how to make do, absolutely, but devote time and resources to investing in the proper tools for the job whenever possible.

## STRESS RESPONSE

Knowing how your body is wired to respond to an emergency can help you see what's coming and react accordingly.

Let's say you detect a sudden, immediate threat, such as a car

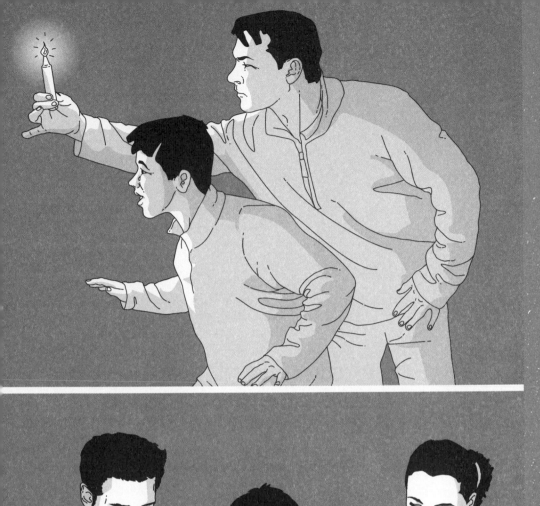

flying around the corner and is heading toward you. Your eyes and ears send information to the amygdala in your brain. That's what interprets the stimuli and makes the decision that danger is imminent. It sends a signal to the hypothalamus. Among other things, the hypothalamus controls your autonomic nervous system functions, such as heartbeat, blood pressure, and breathing. In this case, it is ringing an alarm and telling the adrenal glands to kick into gear. They dump epinephrine, also known as adrenaline, into the bloodstream.

Your heart begins to beat much faster, delivering more blood to your organs and muscles. Your blood pressure will also increase. Oxygen to the lungs is increased due to both heavy breathing as well as airways dilating. All of this serves to sharpen your senses, getting you ready for action. The adrenaline will also free up glucose from where it is stored in the body, converting it to energy.

Because more blood is going to your head and organs, your hands and feet might feel cold. Your face will probably look and feel flushed.

All of this happens almost instantaneously, getting your body ready to leap out of the way of the oncoming car. But, let's change it around a little. Let's say there's more of an ongoing threat analysis situation, such as you

# FIGHT
## OR FLIGHT

Whether consciously or subconsciously, a decision is made on how to handle a threat. It is often decided in an instant.

*Flight*

There is nothing wrong with deciding that discretion is the better part of valor. Retreat can let you to approach a situation from a different angle, perhaps having taken the time to analyze the best response. Let's be real for a second; the ultimate goal in any dangerous situation is for you and your family to survive to see the next day.

*Fight*

If you go this route, remember that there is no such thing as a fair fight. There is a winner and a loser. Do whatever it takes to end up on the winning side. The adrenaline dump and other hormones racing through your system will help by increasing your strength and speed, as well as reducing your pain sensitivity.

think you're being followed.

In this case, the adrenal glands will start producing cortisol. This is sometimes referred to as the primary stress hormone. It further increases the glucose in the bloodstream, providing even more energy. It also suppresses nonessential body functions, such as digestion, in order to prioritize where that increased energy is put to use.

As amazingly efficient as the body can be with this overall stress response, there are a few drawbacks to keep in mind. One of the most common is a loss of fine motor dexterity. With the adrenaline in your blood, your hands will tremble and shake, as will your legs. Forget about trying some kind of intricate or elaborate martial arts maneuver. Stick to gross body movements as much as possible.

When you're under stress, making complex decisions can be difficult or even impossible. Hopefully you won't be forced to answer trivia questions or solve math equations when disaster hits.

CHAPTER 13

# THE FIRST 24 HOURS

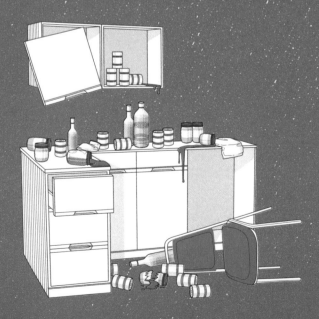

**HOW YOU HANDLE THE FIRST FEW HOURS AFTER A DISASTER STRIKES COULD MAKE THE DIFFERENCE BETWEEN SUCCESS OR FAILURE. THIS IS A CRITICAL TIME FRAME. YOU NEED TO UNDERSTAND SOME OF THE MAIN OBJECTIVES WELL IN ADVANCE, SO YOU'RE PREPARED TO SURVIVE...AND EVEN THRIVE.**

## GATHER INFORMATION

The scenario you find yourself in is what will dictate the exact chain of events. But even so, there are a few things you'll want to get a handle on as quickly as is reasonable.

In order to make informed decisions, you need information to act upon. Fortunately, there are several resources to explore on this front, such as amateur radio or social media. (see Chapter 6). The National Oceanic and Atmospheric Administration (NOAA) radio broadcasts, which we commonly just refer to as "weather radio," can be used to transmit more than just snowfall predictions. They have partnered with the Emergency

Alert System to send out critical information during a crisis situation. For this reason, make sure any emergency radio you purchase is equipped to tune into NOAA broadcasts.

As you tune in to your favorite radio and TV stations, keep in mind that in the early stages of a disaster, news reports get about as much wrong as they do right. Each station wants to be the first to break a story or reveal new information and, in their rush to do so, they'll sometimes report rumors as fact. Social media can be even worse, especially because there's little recourse when someone shares incorrect information.

All other things being equal, urban areas will tend to get attention from the authorities quicker than rural locations, simply because there are more people involved who will need help. While that's great for city dwellers, you still can't count on aid workers knocking on your door in just a couple of hours. However, they're probably on the way.

Do what you can to consult a variety of information sources. Piece things together to try to obtain a true picture of what's happening around you. Use this information to plan a course of action that makes sense.

## ASSESS RESOURCES

As you examine what's going on and determine the extent of the crisis, you should also take stock of your individual situation.

• Is anyone injured or otherwise in need of medical attention?

• Is your home safe, or has it been damaged?

• How much food, water, and other necessary supplies do you have on hand?

Answers to those questions should help you determine what to do next. Obviously, if your home is no longer stable or safe, you'll need to

# HELPING
## OTHERS

If you're able to do so, reach out to neighbors and see how they're faring. Especially in the case of the elderly or infirm, they might not be in a position to do a whole lot on their own. Make sure they are safe and have food and water. Help them get in touch with family members, if need be. Do whatever you can to assist. That's just the right thing to do.

Of course, that means paying attention and actually knowing who lives next door, down the hall, and across the street. This, unfortunately, has been on the wane in recent years. So make it a point to get to know the people who live around you before disaster strikes.

figure out where else you can spend the night, whether that means a local motel, "couchsurfing" with a friend, or heading out of town to a visit a family member for a while.

As for food and other resources, even the most well-prepared preppers could suddenly find themselves lacking due to fire or another calamity. If that were to happen, you'll need a plan for where you're getting your next meal and keeping your family fed.

Of course, when someone is in need of medical help, if you're unable to assist them yourself, you'll need to figure out where you can take them and how you'll get there. The information you're monitoring via radio, television, social media, and other means will hopefully guide you in this regard.

## DEAL WITH PERISHABLES

As we mentioned in Chapter 2, unless food has been contaminated (exposure to flood water, for example, which itself may contain sewage), it won't go bad instantly. However, the clock is ticking from the moment there is no power.

Eat and drink what you can before it goes bad, and preserve what you're able to can or dehydrate. Do this before you dig into whatever special survival food you might have stored away. Make use of everything you can before it goes to waste.

Anything that isn't able to be consumed should be removed from the home and tossed out as soon as possible. Doing so will help prevent foul odors as well as the growth of mold. Vegetables and fruits could be tossed into the compost pile, if you have one. Meats, dairy, and similar items should be put into heavy-duty trash bags and sealed tightly, then be put out for pick up on trash day. Even if the garbage removal services aren't currently running, you don't want these bags sitting around inside your home. They'll attract all kinds of bugs and vermin. Get them out of there and put them somewhere else, ideally well away from your home or building, until they can be disposed of properly.

## DOCUMENTATION

Assuming it isn't some kind of world-ending event, you'll probably be filing a claim with your insurance company for damages. Once everyone in the family is safe, warm, and fed, start documenting everything. Take photos and video of any damage to your home and your possessions. When you're using video, narrate what you're seeing to make it easy for later viewers to understand. With photos, take them from multiple angles whenever possible.

If at all feasible, upload the photos and video footage to some kind of cloud storage as soon as possible. This way, if your phone or camera runs out of power or ends up damaged, you won't lose all your hard work. Lacking any other options, you could send the files to yourself using whatever email provider you have loaded on your smart phone.

Get in touch with your insurance agent as soon as you can. If you can get online, you might be able to start the claim process that way. Even if you're able to do that, you should call your agent to find out if they have any specific suggestions or instructions for you, given the nature of the disaster. They might be able to hook you up with some immediate assistance for shelter, meals, and more.

## CLEAN UP

When practical, get started with putting things back in order. While you might not be able to take care of everything right away, anything you can do now will be beneficial. Outside, there may be downed branches or trees that can be removed, provided you have the right equipment. There may be other debris as well, such as broken pieces from a neighbor's patio set.

If you're dealing with water damage inside the home, such as from sewage overflow or flooding, it is crucial you get things dried out as soon as you can. The longer things remain sodden, the more problems you'll have with mold and mildew. Those can develop in as little as 24 hours and can have many health risks, such as skin irritation and respiratory problems. Make sure you wear latex or nitrile gloves and a good face mask or respirator when dealing with mold.

If mold is indeed visible, don't bring in fans to dry the home. That will just spread spores and increase the problem. Instead, open windows for mild air circulation. Remove wet furniture, carpeting, bedding, and anything else that got soaked. The idea here is to get rid of anything that will continue to contribute to the level of moisture in the home. If ceiling tiles or drywall are water-damaged, pull them down and get them out of the house.

Hard surfaces such as countertops can be cleaned with hot water and a nonammonia-base cleanser. Then, disinfect them with a 10 percent bleach solution. This is why the cleanser should have no ammonia. Mixing bleach with ammonia will create dangerous fumes. Let the bleach solution sit on the surface for several minutes, then rinse it off with clean water.

With porous materials such as rugs, books, and blankets, if you aren't sure whether they have been contaminated by mold, assume they are and get rid of them.

When you talk to your insurance agent, ask if a professional cleaning service would be covered by your policy. If so, get one lined up ASAP. Even if you're able to hire a service, don't sit on your hands while you're waiting. Do anything you can to get the cleaning process started yourself.

## MISSION CRITICAL

The actions you take in the first 24 hours after disaster hits are critical. Plan ahead so you know what needs to happen. You can then prioritize and delegate as appropriate to get it all handled properly.

# CLEANING
# SUPPLIES
## CHECKLIST

Many homes will have most of these items on hand just as a matter of course. However, you might consider setting some aside with your disaster supplies, just in case.

- Bleach
- Nonammonia-base cleanser
- Rags
- Sponges
- Scrub brushes
- Old toothbrushes
- Mops
- Buckets
- Brooms
- Wet/dry vac
- Gloves (latex or nitrile)
- Heavy-duty trash bags

You might want a clothesline and some clothespins as well. If you have someplace to string it up, you can then use it to help dry wet items.

# APPENDIX

WE USE THE TERM "SURVIVAL KITS" AS A KIND OF SHORTHAND, BUT IN DOING SO IT SOMETIMES GIVES THE WRONG IMPRESSION. AT THE CORE, THESE KITS ARE MERELY AN ASSEMBLAGE OF EQUIPMENT AND SUPPLIES PRIMARILY INTENDED FOR A CRISIS. WHERE PEOPLE SOMETIMES STUMBLE IS THINKING THAT THE EQUIPMENT MUST BE PACKAGED ALL TOGETHER IN SOME SORT OF TACTICAL-LOOKING BACKPACK AND BE READY TO STORM THE GATES OF HELL OR SOMETHING SIMILAR.

Or people think that all of these various items must be purchased new, and be top of the line in terms of price. Doing so would probably cost hundreds or more and that alone can leave the impression that survival is somehow only fit for well-to-do people.

The reality is that most of the items in these kits are probably in your home already and can be borrowed from the pantry shelves, or wherever they maybe found, and redesignated for emergency use.

As for how to store the kits, that's up to you. Use whatever is convenient, practical, and makes sense. For example, the workplace kit is something that you'll hide away in a locker or under your desk. It does not need to be a backpack as you probably won't be toting it anywhere. A simple large, sturdy shopping bag or a duffel bag will do the job well.

As a general rule, make it a point to unpack and fully inspect each kit at least twice a year. This is an opportunity to rotate food supplies and batteries as well as be sure everything that's supposed to be there is still present.

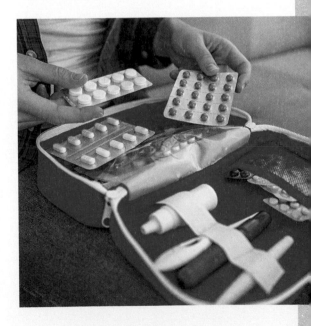

## WORKPLACE EMERGENCY KIT

There are any number of reasons why you might end up stuck at work after hours, from weather problems to civil unrest to just plain old vehicle trouble. While it isn't ideal, given that most of us can't wait for that clock to hit quitting time so we can get out of there, sometimes staying put for a while is your safest option.

The idea behind this kit isn't so much actual survival as it is just making yourself more comfortable. Depending on your workplace, you can keep the kit in your locker or perhaps under your desk or in a corner of your cubicle. Just a simple cloth shopping bag will suffice for a container, which also won't draw undue attention.

## FOOD

While many workplaces are equipped with a breakroom, complete with microwave and other amenities, assume the worst and that you not be able to heat things up. Stick with shelf-stable foods that you can just unwrap and eat. You're not stocking up for the long haul. Think snacks rather than full meals. A few examples:

☐ Dried fruit

☐ Roasted/salted nuts

☐ Granola bars

☐ Cash and coins for vending machines

## WATER

Playing devil's advocate, assume the faucets in the bathroom won't be working.

☐ Bottled water (3-4)

## CLOTHING

If you're stuck at your desk for hours on end at night, you might as well be comfortable. These are just suggestions, tailor them to your own preferences.

☐ Hooded sweatshirt

☐ Thick, soft socks

☐ Soft blue jeans or similar pants

☐ Sneakers

### FLASHLIGHT

Trust me, you'll be the hero of the office during a power outage if you can provide an easy way for people to find their way to and from the bathroom.

- ☐ Flashlights (2) – one for you and one you can lend out

- ☐ Batteries – one extra set for each flashlight

### TOILETRIES

Being able to brush your teeth and wash up a bit will be appreciated by everyone.

- ☐ Toothbrush

- ☐ Toothpaste

- ☐ Dental floss

- ☐ Washcloth

- ☐ Small bar of your favorite soap

- ☐ Feminine hygiene products

## FIRST AID

Most workplaces have at least one first-aid kit, but it never hurts to put one together for yourself. Some content suggestions:

- ☐ Pain relievers
- ☐ Adhesive bandages (various sizes)
- ☐ Gauze pads (various sizes)
- ☐ Medications for stomach ailments
- ☐ Burn cream
- ☐ Antibiotic ointment
- ☐ Cloth tape
- ☐ Antiseptic wipes
- ☐ Nonlatex gloves

## BOREDOM RELIEVERS

If you're stuck at work, the last thing you'll want to do is more work. Assuming the worst and you can't surf social media endlessly to pass the time, you'll want to have a few things to occupy yourself. If nothing else, they might save you from having to endure conversations with coworkers you'd rather avoid. Suggestions include:

- ☐ Books or magazines to read
- ☐ Puzzle books (word find, crossword, Sudoku)
- ☐ Deck of cards

## RELAXATION

If you end up stuck for more than a few hours, you might want to find a quiet area where you can nap.

- ☐ Inflatable pillow
- ☐ Small blanket

## VEHICLE EMERGENCY KIT

Several years ago, a blizzard hit south-central Wisconsin. The timing couldn't have been worse, coming in the late afternoon as people were commuting home. A couple of semitrucks slid around and ended up blocking an interstate highway, backing up traffic for miles. The snow was coming down so hard that it wasn't until the next morning that the authorities were able to get the road opened.

Hundreds of vehicles, and their occupants, were stuck where they were all night long.

The purpose behind this kit is to get you back on the road if something goes awry, or if that's not feasible, to keep you safe and comfortable until help arrives. What works well for storing the kit is a plastic clothes basket in the trunk. Most of these items will fit into the basket and it will keep it all from rolling around.

## TOOLS

The unfortunate reality is that there might not be a whole lot of repair work you can do on the side of the road with a newer vehicle. However, having these items with you can be helpful.

- ☐ Spare tire (check for inflation on a regular basis)
- ☐ Jack
- ☐ Four-way tire iron
- ☐ Tire inflater and sealant
- ☐ Portable jump starter (keep it charged)
- ☐ Assorted fuses
- ☐ Repair manual for your vehicle
- ☐ Coolant (1 gallon)
- ☐ Motor oil (2-3 quarts /2–3 liters)
- ☐ Tire pressure gauge
- ☐ Duct tape
- ☐ Sharp knife
- ☐ Adjustable wrench
- ☐ Screwdrivers (flathead, Phillips head, Torx)
- ☐ Flashlight and/or LED headlamp
- ☐ Flares and/or orange triangle reflectors

## ELECTRONICS

If the car's battery is dead, you won't be able to use the vehicle to charge your phone or other devices. While the portable jump starter might have that capability, there's little harm in picking up a small power pack to keep in the glove box.

- ☐ Power bank for cell phone
- ☐ Charging cable

## TRACTION AIDS

If you live in an area that regularly gets snow and ice in the winter, there's always a risk of getting stuck and your tires just spinning on slick surfaces. Plus, the added weight of one of these in the trunk can help keep you on the road.

- ☐ Cat litter
- ☐ Sand

## COMFORT ITEMS

If you're stuck for a while, you'll want to have the means to make yourself comfortable.

- ☐ Blankets (emergency, and one for each seat)
- ☐ Bottled water (6 bottles)
- ☐ Shelf-stable snack food

## HIKING EMERGENCY KIT

One of the best things you can do for physical and mental health is to get outside regularly. Hiking need not be a contest for distance or speed. Just getting fresh air and sunshine can work wonders. Of course, hitting the trail isn't without risk. You could take a wrong turn and end up absolutely lost. Or you could twist an ankle or knee to such a degree that you're effectively stranded.

The contents of this kit won't keep you alive for weeks or months. The goal is just to get you through a night or two until you can either self-rescue or someone is able to find you. Most of these items can be kept in your pockets or carried in a belt pouch.

### SHELTER

Exposure can and will kill if you're not careful. You need to maintain your core body temperature in order to avoid hypothermia or worse.

- ☐ Emergency blanket
- ☐ Cordage (to aid in building an expedient shelter)

### FIRE MAKING

Fire will warm you up, dry you out, and help you feel better about the overall situation. Don't rely on primitive methods; take advantage of the modern conveniences available as much as possible.

- ☐ Disposable lighters
- ☐ Ferrocerium rod and striker
- ☐ Fresnel lens
- ☐ Tinder

### WATER

You should always have a filled water bottle with you when you start your hike, because hydration is important. But you should also have the means to purify additional water, should your trip ends up taking far longer than you planned.

- ☐ Water bottle (2L)
- ☐ Water purification tablets
- ☐ Coffee filters (to remove sediment from the water before purifying)

### FOOD

You can survive several days without food, though it won't be fun to do so. However, if you're not bringing a full backpack, space is limited. Choose a few things that will keep your stomach from growling constantly. It wouldn't hurt to bring a few things that will help you acquire food in the wild, too.

- ☐ Granola bars
- ☐ Trail mix
- ☐ Fruit (fresh or dried)
- ☐ Fishing line
- ☐ Fish hooks

## NAVIGATION

Being able to find your way home will obviously keep you from being lost. Of course, just having these items isn't enough; you need to learn how to use them effectively.

☐ Compass

☐ GPS-enabled device

☐ Map of the local area

## FIRST-AID KIT

You won't be carrying much, so stick to the bare essentials.

☐ Pain relievers

☐ Adhesive bandages

☐ Medical tape

☐ Gauze pads

☐ Packet of hand wipes

## TOOLS

Again, you're trying to keep things lightweight, so just a couple of things that will be helpful.

☐ Sharp knife

☐ Small flashlight

## SIGNALING

If you end up lost or stranded, you'll want ways you can help people find you quickly. If your cell phone isn't working, you'll have to attract someone another way.

☐ Personal locator beacon (really only needed if you're headed way off the beaten path)

☐ Signal mirror

☐ Whistle

## EVACUATION KIT

Also called a bug-out bag, the goal is to have a pack or bag packed and ready to go, just in case something happens that makes you decide to flee your home in a hurry. This isn't "run to the woods to live off the land" survival kit. Instead, the idea is to provide for your basic needs for a short time while you shelter with a friend or at a motel for a while.

Keep this bag in an out of the way, yet easily accessed location, such as at the back of a closet near the front door. It is not a bad idea for each family member to have their own bag, to help split up the load.

Also worth noting is that you should already have your vehicle emergency kit loaded and thus you'll have access to those supplies in addition to this evacuation kit.

## ESSENTIALS

If you absolutely must leave home with nothing else, make sure you have these items with you.

☐ Cell phone with power bank charger and cord

☐ Wallet with cash, credit cards, and identification

## CLOTHING

You might need to evacuate in whatever you're wearing at the time, which could be your pajamas or even less.

☐ At least one full set of clothes

☐ Extra underwear (2-3)

☐ Extra socks (2-3)

## TOILETRIES

While you might be able to pick these up along the way or once you arrive at your bug-out location, they don't weigh much and don't take up much space. Think along the lines of what you'd need for a weekend trip out of town.

☐ Hairbrush or comb

☐ Toothbrush

☐ Toothpaste

☐ Dental floss

☐ Small bar of soap

☐ Deodorant

## FOOD

It isn't a bad idea to have a mix of snacks as well as a few lightweight camping food options that can provide a more filling meal, if the opportunity warrants. A few examples:

☐ Dehydrated/freeze-dried meals (1-2 per person)

☐ Protein bars

☐ Pouched meats (chicken, tuna)

☐ Instant oatmeal or hot cereal

☐ Instant rice

☐ Ramen noodles

☐ Jerky

☐ Peanut butter

You'll also need utensils and cookware, if you're going beyond ready-to-eat foods, as well as a means of heating water.

☐ Mess kit

☐ Utensils (plastic or metal)

☐ Small camp stove with fuel bottle

☐ Disposable lighters (for lighting the stove)

## WATER

It's heavy and difficult to transport, but you should have some water with you, as well as the means to purify or filter additional water sourced elsewhere.

- ☐ Water bottle (2L), filled, per person
- ☐ Water filter
- ☐ Purification tablets

## NAVIGATION

You should have already selected one or more potential bug-out locations, so it is just a matter of knowing how you'll get to them.

- ☐ Maps of the area
- ☐ List of motels and phone numbers
- ☐ List of phone numbers for friends and family members

## MEDICAL

You might not have the time to stop to pick anything up right away, so make sure you have the basics packed ahead of time.

- ☐ First-aid kit
- ☐ Prescription medications (at least one week's supply)

## TOOLS AND EQUIPMENT

Remember, the plan here isn't to head off to the mountains and become a hermit until the end of time. You're just heading out of town for a while until it is safe to return home. That said, there are a couple of things that should be present in every survival kit, due to their usefulness.

- ☐ Flashlight and/or headlamp
- ☐ Sharp knife
- ☐ Duct tape

## MISCELLANEOUS

There are a few other odds and ends that you should keep in your bug-out bag that might make things easier for you and your family.

- ☐ List of important phone numbers, in case your cell phone isn't available
- ☐ Flash drive with scanned copies of important documents and photos
- ☐ Small portable radio to keep up on news if you're stuck somewhere

## APPENDIX B
## THE SURVIVAL LIBRARY

No individual reference book could ever hope to cover every single topic in exhaustive detail when it comes to prepping. Building a collection of books and other materials at home is a great way to ensure you have vital information at your fingertips. It is recommended to have physical hard copies whenever possible. While yes, they will require some amount of storage space, they'll prove to be worth their weight in gold if you are not able to access e-copies stored in the cloud somewhere.

What follows are suggestions for additional reading as well as solid recommendations for additions to your survival library. While you're free to collect them all, don't feel that is absolutely necessary. However, it isn't a bad idea to pick up at least a couple in each category, just for varying points of view.

### GENERAL PREPAREDNESS

*Practical Self-Reliance* by John D. McCann (John D. McCann, 2014)

*Be Ready for Anything* by Daisy Luther (Racehorse Publishing, 2019)

*The Prepper's Workbook* by Scott Williams and Scott Finazzo (Ulysses Press, 2020)

*The Prepper's Pocket Guide* by Bernie Carr (Ulysses Press, 2011)

*Build the Perfect Bug Out Bag* by Creek Stewart (Krause Publications, 2012)

*Build the Perfect Survival Kit* by John McCann (2nd edition, Living Ready Magazine, 2013)

*Prepper's Long-Term Survival Guide* by Jim Cobb (Ulysses Press, 2014)

*Prepper's Complete Book of Disaster Readiness* by Jim Cobb (Ulysses Press, 2013)

### HOMESTEADING AND GARDENING

*The Encyclopedia of Country Living* by Carla Emery (Sasquatch Books, 2019)

*Storey's Basic Country Skills* by John and Martha Storey (Storey Publishing, LLC, 1999)

*The Mini Farming Bible* by Brett Markham (Skyhorse Publishing, 2014)

*Creating the Low-Budget Homestead* by Steven Gregersen (Independently published, 2018)

*Curious Compendium of Practical and Obscure Skills* by The How-To Experts (Storey Publishing, LLC, 2020)

## WILD EDIBLES

*Peterson Field Guide to Medicinal Plants and Herbs of Eastern and Central North America* (3rd edition, Mariner Books, 2014)

*Guide to Wild Foods and Useful Plants* by Christopher Nyerges (2nd Edition, Chicago Review Press, 2014)

*Foraging Wild Edibles Plants of North America* by Christopher Nyerges (Falcon Guides, 2016)

## MEDICAL

*The Survival Medicine Handbook* by Dr. Joseph Alton and Amy Alton, ARNP 4th edition, Doom and Bloom, LLC, 2021)

*Alton's Antibiotics and Infectious Disease* by Dr. Joseph Alton and Amy Alton, ARNP (Alton First Aid LLC, 2018)

*Prepper's Natural Medicine* by Cat Ellis (Ulysses Press, 2015)

## MINDSET

*The Unthinkable* by Amanda Ripley (Harmony, 2009)

*The Gift of Fear* by Gavin de Becker (Bantam Doubleday Dell Publishing Group, 2007)

*Left of Bang* by Patrick Van Horne and Jason Riley (Black Irish Entertainment LLC, 2014)

## WILDERNESS SURVIVAL

*Extreme Wilderness Survival* by Craig Caudill (Page Street Publishing, 2017)

*Stay Alive* by John D. McCann (Krause Publications, 2011)

*Ultimate Wilderness Gear* by Craig Caudill (Page Street Publishing, 2018)

*101 Skills You Need to Survive in the Woods* by Kevin Estela (Page Street Publishing, 2019)

*Bushcraft Basics* by Leon Pantenburg (Skyhorse Publishing, 2020)

*Bushcraft 101* by Dave Canterbury (Adams Media, 2014)

*Surviving the Wild* by Joshua Enyart (Mango Publishing, 2021)

*Build the Perfect Bug Out Skills* by Creek Stewart (Living Ready Magazine, 2015)

*Ninja Wilderness Survival Guide* by Hakim Isler (Tuttle Publishing, 2021)

*Wilderness Adventure Camp: Essential Outdoor Survival Skills for Kids* by Frank Grindrod (Storey Publishing, LLC, 2021)

## APPENDIX C
## RECOMMENDED SUPPLIERS

There are so many companies out there operating in the survival and prepper niche, it can be difficult to determine which are offering high-quality products and which are just fly-by-night companies looking to make a fast buck.

To that end, I wanted to share my own favorite manufacturers and suppliers. I've personally done business with every single company listed here. I've used their products and recommend them wholeheartedly. To be clear, I don't work for any of them; I don't have any kind of affiliate arrangement with any of them, and they certainly aren't paying me anything to be included in this list.

I've included the website for each company, but you should definitely check local sources for gear and equipment to see if they carry the brand(s) that you're interested in.

### COMMUNICATION
Kaito: Kaitoradio.com

Midland: Midlandusa.com

### FIRST AID / MEDICAL
Adventure Medical Kits: Adventuremedicalkits.com

Doom and Bloom: Store. doomandbloom.net

### FLASHLIGHTS
Fenix: Fenixlighting.com

Streamlight: Streamlight.com

Thrunite: Thrunite.com

### KNIVES
Most of the listed brands can be found at my preferred knife distributor, DLT Trading (dlttrading. com). They are happy to ship internationally, too.

Bark River Knives: Barkriverknives. com

Benchmade: Benchmade.com

Case Knives: Caseknives.com

CRKT: Crkt.com

D. Tope Knives: Facebook.com/ dtopeknives

Kershaw: Kershaw.kaiusa.com

TOPS Knives: Topsknives.com

Victorinox: Victorinox.com

Vehement Knives: Vehementknives. com

White River Knives: Whiteriverknives. com

## MULTITOOLS
Leatherman: Leatherman.com

SOG: Sogknives.com

## PACKS, BAGS, POUCHES
5.11 Tactical: 511Tactical.com

Eberlestock: Eberlestock.com

Maxpedition: Maxpedition.com

Rothco: Rothco.com

The Hidden Woodsmen: Thehiddenwoodsmen.com

Tuff Possum Gear: Tuffpossumgear. com

Vanquest: Vanquest.com

Vertx: Vertx.com

Yellow Birch Outfitters: Yellowbirchoutfitters.com

## PORTABLE ENERGY
Goal Zero: Goalzero.com

Jackery: Jackery.com

## SURVIVAL KITS AND COMPONENTS
Exotac: Exotac.com

Stanford Outdoor Supply: Stanfordoutdoorsupply.com

Survive Outdoors Longer (SOL): Surviveoutdoorslonger.com

Sustain Supply: Sustain.com

Wazoo Survival Gear: Wazoosurvivalgear.com

## WATER TREATMENT
Berkey Filters: Berkeyfilters.com

GRAYL : Grayl.com

Katadyn: Katadyngroup.com

MSR: Msrgear.com

Sawyer: Sawyer.com

# INDEX

## ACKNOWLEDGEMENTS

While writing is generally a solitary activity, it cannot be properly done in a vacuum. It takes input and support from a range of people. I love having the opportunity to recognize and acknowledge those who have helped get me where I am today, but part of me hates doing this as human nature is to forget someone along the way. So, apologies in advance for any inadvertent omissions.

First and foremost, huge thanks to my beautiful and brilliant wife Tammy. Quite literally, I'd have never made it this far as an author without your support and guidance, as well as pushing me to be the best man I can be.

To my sons, Andrew, Michael, and Thomas, you are each growing up to be wonderful young men and I can't wait to see where you go from here.

To Chris Golden and Brian Keene, thank you for helping me to avoid pitfalls and for always being a source for advice as well as inspiration.

To Pete Orndorff, thank you for listening to me complain from time to time. People!

To Mike McCourt, I loved working with you over the last several years and I'm hopeful we'll have the opportunity to do so again someday.

To my knife family – Mike Stewart and the Bark River crew, Matt and Jenna Martin, Dan Tope, and Jason Thoune and the DLT Trading team – thank you so much for your support and your friendship. I promise I'll make it back up for a Grind-In soon!

To John McCann, you've taught me so much over the years and I truly appreciate everything you've done for me.

To Craig Caudill, I cannot say thank you enough for your  invaluable support and friendship.

Last but not least, tremendous thanks to Malcolm Croft and Katie Baxendale and everyone else at Welbeck Publishing (with honorable mention to Chris Mitchell, too). The partnership at every step of the process has been nothing short of awesome. I truly appreciate it.

# CREDITS

The publishers would like to thank the following sources for their kind permission to reproduce the pictures in this book.

t-top, b-bottom, l-left, r-right

Alamy: Allstar Picture Library Ltd 122; Oliver Dixon 107; Richard Levine 10; Reuters 72

Courtesy Jim Cobb: 51, 121, 123t, 123b, 124t, 124b, 125, 126

Getty Images: AFP 9; Gallo Images 54r; Hector Mata 13; Matt Moyer 127

Shutterstock: Radg Aivazoff 23b; Potashev Aleksandr 219; ArtCookStudio 143; Art_Pictures 69; Yaroslav Astakhov 205; Evgeny Atamanenko 189; Michael Barajas 176; Baza Production 30b; BearFotos 66; bgrocker 171b; Billion Photos 73; Kris Black 85; Black Jack 103; Mr. Aekalak Chiamcharoen 151b; ChiccoDodiFC 185tr; Cookie Studio 113; Cultura Creative RF 215t; Benoit Daoust 145b; Davizro Photography 21b; dcwcreations 115; DimaBerlin 60; Oleg Doroshin 45, 142; Aubord Dulac 111b; Dziegler 59; Amada Ekeli 47; Timothy Epp 27; EugeneEdge 58; Everett Collection 7; FStockLuk 197; fizkes 117, 162, 165b, 188; FotoDuets 141; Nor Gal 128; Gardens by Design 40t; Dan Gerber 195; Gerisima 138l; goffkein.pro 203; Dragana Gordic 108; Kaspars Grinvalds 92; guruXOX 101; Hal_P 110; Keith Homan 26; igorfrontier 169; Diane Isabel 133t; John D. Ivanko 131; JazzyGeoff 99; Juice Flair 151t; Simon Kadula 52t; Oleksandr Kliuiko 28; Przemek Klos 75;

Robert Kneschke 78, 140; Art Konovalov 135b; Teerasak Ladnongkhun 149; lajulia19 172; Lazy_Bear 83t; lightpoet 61; Lopolo 63; loreanto 65b; Lotus_studio 23t; Olivia Lunar 198; MagicBones Alexander Maksimov 111t; Riccardo Mayer 33; Mega Pixel 81; MikeDotta 173; Monticello 167, 212; nata-lunata 55; New Africa 42, 71, 83b, 156; Odua Images 50; paintings 200; Sasirin Pamai 145t; Peerayot 187; /David Pereiras 178, 180, 185tl, 185b; photolike 40br; Photographer_of_nature 38; Photographicss 91b; Phovoir 136; Picsfive 77; Pixsooz 89; Andrey_Popov 138r; Poring Studio 82; Pressmaster 211; Radowitz 37; Raland 52b; Rawpixel.com 153; Jeerayut Rianwed 40bl; Rido 206b; RollingCamera 80; Howard Sayer 104; Elena Schweitzer 54l; Sean Locke Photography 182; Sentelia 35; Sergio Sergo 21t; Adrian Sherratt 208; SpeedKingz 193; DJ Taylor 22; SpicyTruffel 132-133b; Studio Romantic 166; tommaso79 65t; Tonelson Productions 18; topimages 68; Triff 79; urbanbuzz 129; VH-studio 48; Vaks-stock Agency 171t; Vintage Tone 147; Vitalii Vodolazskyi 159; Wayhome 206t; studio 148; Yeti studio 137; Dmytro Zinkevych 91t, 207

All illustrations: Peter Liddiard

Every effort has been made to acknowledge correctly and contact the source and/or copyright holder of each picture and Welbeck Publishing apologises for any unintentional errors or omissions, which will be corrected in future editions of this book.